OXFORD WORLD'S CLASSICS

====

COLETTE

The Cat and The Masked Woman

====

Translated by
HELEN CONSTANTINE

with an Introduction and Notes by
DIANA HOLMES

OXFORD
UNIVERSITY PRESS

OXFORD
UNIVERSITY PRESS

Great Clarendon Street, Oxford, OX2 6DP,
United Kingdom

Oxford University Press is a department of the University of Oxford.
It furthers the University's objective of excellence in research, scholarship,
and education by publishing worldwide. Oxford is a registered trade mark of
Oxford University Press in the UK and in certain other countries

Translation © Helen Constantine 2025
Introduction and Notes © Diana Holmes 2025
Chronology © Paul Gibbard 2025

The moral rights of the authors have been asserted

Published in the United States of America by Oxford University Press
198 Madison Avenue, New York, NY 10016, United States of America

British Library Cataloguing in Publication Data

Data available

Library of Congress Control Number: 2024949135

ISBN 9780198863724

Printed and bound in the UK by
Clays Ltd, Elcograf S.p.A.

Links to third party websites are provided by Oxford in good faith and
for information only. Oxford disclaims any responsibility for the materials
contained in any third party website referenced in this work.

MIX
Paper | Supporting
responsible forestry
FSC
www.fsc.org   FSC® C018072

The manufacturer's authorised representative in the EU for product safety is
Oxford University Press España S.A. of El Parque Empresarial San Fernando de Henares,
Avenida de Castilla, 2 - 28830 Madrid (www.oup.es/en or product.safety@oup.com
OUP España S.A. also acts as importer into Spain of products made by the manufacturer.

CONTENTS

INTRODUCTION

Readers new to the stories should note that this Introduction makes details of the plots explicit.

COLETTE falls outside the classic narrative of French literary history, which contains very few women. She belonged to no literary school or movement, and her work's popular appeal, especially to female readers, excluded it from critical esteem for parts of the literary establishment. For decades during and after her lifetime, she was acknowledged to be an exquisite stylist, but her themes and plots were deemed by many to be trivial, frivolous, or even tawdry: 'Having read the book with delight, on account of the beauty of the writing, we doubt if we shall open it again because there is so little in it', as one review of *La Chatte,* in the *Times Literary Supplement* (*TLS*), put it in 1933.[1] The literary critic Nicole Ward-Jouve, who was a serious-minded schoolgirl in the France of the 1950s, remembers being discouraged from reading Colette by the image of her as a 'fanciful and shallow' writer who only wrote about 'frivolous feminine things, love and plants and animals and her family'.[2] Meanwhile, Colette's work was being carefully filleted to extract morally unexceptionable passages of descriptive prose for school dictations, designed to exemplify the wonder of the French language without endangering the morals of the young. Generations of post-war French children grew up associating Colette with the torture of trying to spell exotic names of flowers and trees.

There were always, however, critics as well as enthusiastic readers who recognized that the beauty of the writing was inseparable from an original and compelling vision of the world, and this is the evaluation of Colette that now, in the twenty-first century, has largely prevailed. Thanks not least to feminist literary criticism—both French and anglophone—from the 1970s on, that brought into focus her singularly woman-centric perspective on reality, Colette is now widely

---

[1] Quoted in Margaret Callender, *Le Blé en herbe* and *La Chatte* (Critical Guides to French Texts; London: Grant & Cutler, 1992), 53.

[2] Nicole Ward-Jouve, *Colette* (Bloomington: Indiana University Press, 1987), 2.

acknowledged to be one of the greatest French authors of the modern period. Her work is published in four volumes in the prestigious Pléiade edition; she is the subject of a substantial body of critical work, and acclaimed as one of Julia Kristeva's three 'female geniuses' alongside Hannah Arendt and Simone de Beauvoir.[3] The 150th anniversary of her birth in 2023 was extensively celebrated, in France and across the world.

Her life as well as her writing make her a vivid twentieth-century heroine. Her biography, especially that of her early life, is well known, woven into her own genre-defying auto-fictional work, recounted in numerous biographies and in Wash Westmoreland's critically and commercially successful 2018 biopic *Colette*. She was born in 1873 in the Burgundy village of Saint-Sauveur-en-Puisaye, which now houses a Colette museum and study centre. Her mother, Sidonie Colette or 'Sido', would become in her daughter's work a sort of secular deity, a model of nurturing yet dissident femininity; her father, Jules Colette, was a one-legged ex-soldier with unrealized literary ambitions, who also appears in some of Colette's writing as a sympathetically eccentric character. The youngest of four children, Colette enjoyed an unconventionally free and happy girlhood that ended with her family's bankruptcy and—given the paucity of feasible female destinies in late nineteenth-century France—with marriage at the age of 20 to Henri Gauthier-Villars, known as Willy, fourteen years her senior and a sophisticated, libidinous Parisian man-about-town. The move to Paris was both life-expanding—Willy moved in the cultured, bohemian circles of the fin de siècle demi-monde—and distressing, as the young wife soon discovered her husband's serial infidelities. But it was also to be the start of Colette's literary career. Willy could be described as a literary entrepreneur, the 'author' of popular, risqué novels in fact written by a stable of ghostwriters, and it was his injunction to write down her memories of schooldays that launched Colette—albeit under Willy's signature—into writing. The *Claudine* novels, fictionalized versions of Colette's own girlhood and youth, bore the stamp of Willy's lascivious imagination but are also unmistakably Colettian, with their lyrical evocations of the natural

---

[3] Colette, *Œuvres* (Paris: Bibliothèque de la Pléiade, Gallimard, 1986–2001); Julia Kristeva, *Le Génie féminin*, iii. *Colette* (Paris: Fayard, 2002); trans. into English by Jane Marie Todd as *Colette* (Columbia: Columbia University Press, 2004).

world, irreverent humour, and passionate sensuality. They became huge bestsellers. However when the couple separated in 1906, all the income from the books (and associated merchandise—Willy had a good eye for the market) went to their official author and Colette had to find other ways of making a living. She trained as a mime and dancer, went on the music-hall stage—and continued to write.

The last of the five Claudine novels, *La Retraite sentimentale* (The Retreat from Love) was published in 1907 after the couple's separation and bids farewell to Claudine in Colette's own unadorned voice; *Les Vrilles de la vigne* (The Tendrils of the Vine) followed, a collection of short pieces that mixed fiction; some deft, often comical animal sketches; and life-writing, including lyrical evocations of Colette's relationship with her lesbian lover, 'Missy', Mathilde de Mornay, Marquise de Belbeuf. *La Vagabonde*, published in 1910, fictionalized its author's own life through the story of Renée Néré, a divorced 'woman of letters who has turned out badly',[4] earning her living on the music-hall stage but still passionately drawn to writing ('a need, sharp as thirst in summer, to note and to describe'[5]), proudly independent but painfully aware that for a woman of her time, freedom is incompatible with heterosexual love. For though Colette was still with Missy, she was also engaged in an affair with a wealthy, handsome young man who almost certainly provided the model for Renée's lover, Max. Like her heroine, Colette liberated herself by performing versions of her identity on stage and on the page, achieving (if only just) financial autonomy and control over her own image. The desire for love triumphed, however, for a time, both in the sequel to Renée's story, the suggestively entitled *L'Entrave* (The Shackle), in which she exchanges the 'vagabond' life of a touring dancer for the role of loving mistress, and in Colette's own life when she fell for Henry de Jouvenel, the handsome editor of one of France's major daily newspapers, *Le Matin*. Finding herself pregnant—at the age of 40— Colette married him, and gave birth to her daughter in 1913. The music-hall days were over, though Colette would continue to tread the boards as an actress, playing some of her own heroines, and as a conference speaker. Her principal role now, though, was as a writer: she became a successful journalist, and from 1914 to 1924 was literary

---

[4] Colette, *The Vagabond*, trans. Enid McLeod (Harmondsworth: Penguin, 1960), 12.
[5] Ibid. 13.

editor of *Le Matin*. During the First World War she volunteered briefly as a nurse in the hospitals set up for wounded soldiers, smuggled herself to the Front to visit the mobilized Henry and report back as a war correspondent, shared a house with women friends in what they called their 'phalanstery' (a word that evokes a utopian model of communal living), and continued to publish fiction and short pieces in the press.

Her second marriage also ended in divorce in 1925, both parties having engaged in extramarital affairs, in Colette's case most scandalously with her teenage stepson Bertrand de Jouvenel. She would go on to write many more novels (including *The Cat*) and auto-fictional texts, as well as stories and articles for newspapers and magazines, and to marry for a third time, to the younger, devoted Maurice Goudeket with whom she remained until her death in 1954. A state funeral marked her accession to the status of 'notre grande Colette', acclaimed public figure and member of the Académie Goncourt. The Catholic Church's refusal to grant her a religious funeral kept alive the aura of scandal that had always surrounded the only famous French author to have danced semi-naked on a stage, engaged in a very public lesbian relationship as well as several heterosexual affairs, divorced two husbands, and portrayed the world from a resolutely female point of view.

Style and Substance

What does it mean to say that Colette is a brilliant stylist, that she writes 'beautifully', as most critics seem to have agreed even when bemoaning the insubstantiality of her plots and themes? It is not hard to see why the writing itself—what the French call, in a word resonant with respect for the written word, Colette's *écriture*—should strike the reader first. Reading Colette is a singularly sensory experience, for her words constantly evoke the visual appearance, textures, and scents of bodies, furnished interiors, gardens, food, with an unusual precision that celebrates the abundant materiality of everyday human life. Julia Kristeva calls Colette's *écriture* an 'interpenetration of language and the world, of style and flesh'.[6] The words themselves both fulfil a descriptive function, effectively evoking

---

[6] Kristeva, *Le Génie féminin*, iii. *Colette*, 15.

a known—or at least an acutely plausible—reality, and offer the sensual pleasure of language as sound and rhythm. Her prose has a musical as well as a poetic quality, captured in the best translations, as here when in one of the stories in *The Masked Woman* a traveller stranded on a cold autumn night is welcomed into a warm, hospitable home:

After some vintage plum brandy and boiling hot coffee, we were almost like old friends. The electric light, rare in that part of the world, the scent of blond tobacco, fruit, the blazing wood smelling of resin—I savoured these homely delights as though they were gifts from an undiscovered island. (p. 94)

or in *The Cat* when we first see the garden of Alain's beloved home, through his eyes:

High in the sky sat a veiled moon, enlarged by the mist of the first warm days. One solitary tree, a poplar with smooth young leaves, captured the bright moonshine and dripped as many gleams as a cascade of water. (p. 5)

And Colette's skill with linguistic form extends to her command of narrative. As the texts in this volume demonstrate, though her fictions favour intimate, personal events rather than plots of dramatic action, she certainly knew how to tell a story: both the short texts assembled in *The Masked Woman* and the short novel *The Cat* display the arts of narrative concision, vivid characterization, and that patterning of fictional time and place that creates tension followed by the release of a conclusion—what one great narrative theorist called the 'tick-tock' of narrative time, as opposed to the mere 'tick tick tick' of everyday lived experience.[7] Colette's command of style and structure certainly deserves acknowledgement in its own right. Yet literary form can surely not be divorced from meaning, and in Colette's case the specific beauty of her writing is impossible to separate from the vision of life that Kristeva termed her 'affirmative genius'.[8]

If Colette creates character primarily through the depiction of bodies, this is not a limitation but rather a means to render perceptible human psychology and those subtle fluctuations of feeling that colour subjective life and relationships. When in the story 'The Other Woman' a couple chance upon the husband's ex-wife, their

---

[7] Frank Kermode, *The Sense of an Ending* (Oxford: Oxford Univeristy Press, 1967), 47.

[8] Kristeva, *Le Génie féminin*, iii. *Colette*, 19.

self-conscious awareness of her presence, and of how she might perceive them, is conveyed almost entirely through bodily gesture: 'Alice
sometimes laughed rather too loud and Marc was careful not to slump
in his chair, pulling back his shoulders and sitting upright' (p. 116).
In *The Cat*, Alain's recoil from his new wife's disruption of his single
life, and its continuity with his cherished childhood, becomes a sense
of repulsion at her dark, sensual body: 'And he was stunned, for
instance, even scandalized, when he realized how dark Camille was'
(p. 42); the sight of one of her black hairs in the sink makes him feel
sick. Colette's world is always embodied, sensory perception inseparable from thought and emotion.

Bodies are equally central to Colette's radical representation of
sex and gender. The male gaze—man as subject of perception and
woman as its object—still dominated literature and art when
Colette, from her earliest writing on, turned her evaluative, sometimes desiring female gaze on men's as well as women's bodies. The
masked woman, in the story of that name, casually kisses the mouth
of a young stranger blessed with a 'handsome, fresh, and brutal'
face (p. 89); Alain as well as Camille has a strong physical presence
in *The Cat*, even though his is the primary narrative point of view.
Camille's physical desire for him—she is moved by the sight of his
lips pressing against the glass as he drinks, troubled by a glimpse of
his naked chest—communicates the erotic appeal of Alain's body to
the reader. This textual subversion of men's appropriation of sub-
jecthood carries through to the whole way that Colette represents
men and women. Both the texts translated here appeared in the
interwar years which in France saw a severe backlash against those
minor liberties won by women under war conditions, and a strong
emphasis on traditional gender roles, marriage, and for women
motherhood. Colette's women are rarely mothers, and Camille (*The
Cat*) is exceptional in envisaging maternity as part of her future.
The stories portray marriage—or more often unmarried couple-
dom—as an often temporary, difficult state that rarely leads to lasting happiness, especially for women but also for men. For if Colette
reverses long-established norms by depicting reality primarily from
a female point of view, she is also interested in male experience and
portrays a strictly binary construction of gender roles as restrictive
and distorting for both sexes. The valuing of Colette's work essen-
tially for its style downplays the extent to which she portrays and

challenges normative values, in a manner that also has wider philosophical implications.

Colette's corporeal style of characterization also relates to her unusual manner of depicting animals, central to *The Cat* but also glimpsed in some of the short stories. Colette situates human beings as part of the natural, material world, so that human exceptionalism—the view that humanity is inherently different and superior to all other living beings—is contested, and humans are physical bodies just as non-human animals display an inner life of perceptions and feelings. The tame little fox in the story named for him, with his 'velvety eyes' and 'beautiful tail the colour of lightly toasted bread' (p. 104), is a vibrant physical presence. But the narrator also recognizes the fox's inner struggle, torn between affectionate loyalty to the man who cares for him and the despair of a wild creature confined by a collar and lead. The brief victory of the animal's carnivorous desire is mirrored in the momentary eruption of instinctive violence in his owner: these two, like Saha the cat and her human companions, exist on a continuum rather than being of unrelated species. The first book Colette published under (more or less) her own name—as Colette Willy—was, significantly, *Dialogues de bêtes* (Animal Dialogues), and it is far from fanciful to see her, as some critics have, as a foremother of ecologism and animal liberation.

Sensuality, a profound feel for the inexhaustible richness of sensation and attendant emotion offered by the material world, is fundamental to Colette's style and communicates an affirmative philosophy of life. 'Regarde!' ('Look!') was, at least in Colette's recreation of her, Sido's principal imperative, and Colette's writing invites close attention to and appreciation of the endless variety of sheer 'thereness' of the world. In *Break of Day* (first published in 1928) she wrote of 'my sensuality whose eyes, thank God, were always bigger than its belly',[9] and her writing is charged with that appetite for life in even its most ordinary, everyday forms that, as Julia Kristeva put it, asserts 'a strange osmosis between sensations, desires and anxieties, those "pleasures too lightly termed physical", and the immeasurable richness of the world'.[10]

---

[9] Colette, *Break of Day* (first published in French, 1928), trans. Enid McLeod (London: The Women's Press, 1979), 28.

[10] Kristeva, *Le Génie féminin*, iii. *Colette*, 13.

The Cat

La Chatte—The Cat—was published in 1933, and written at an extremely busy period of Colette's life. She was living at the Hôtel Claridge in Paris, and in an established relationship with Maurice Goudeket who would become her third husband in 1935. Energetic and creative, and also in a state of constant financial insecurity, Colette combined her prolific career as a writer with regular conference tours, working in the cinema on film subtitling and scriptwriting, pursuing her journalism, including theatre criticism, and, in 1932–3, setting up a beauty salon and a range of 'Colette' beauty products, which also demanded marketing strategies dependent on the author's presence. Little wonder then that in January 1933, writing in between two train journeys, she should exclaim in a letter to her friend Hélène Picard: 'Ouf! At the same time I've been scribbling away at that little novel "The Cat".'[11] 'Scribbling away' conveyed her sense of haste and urgency, but downplayed the extreme, laborious care Colette brought to all her writing, described in *The Vagabond* as 'the patient struggling with a phrase until it becomes supple and finally settles down [...] the motionless lying in wait for a word by which in the end one *ensnares* it'.[12] The novel was finished by the spring and published first in nine episodes in the weekly illustrated magazine *Marianne*, then in June as a book. Reception was mixed. Several critics ardently admired the novel and took Saha the cat to be 'the very incarnation of Mme Colette herself'.[13] Others, such as the author and screenwriter Pierre Bost, lamented the 'odious' and 'ridiculous' nature of the characters and deplored Colette's 'antihumanism',[14] and we have seen that the *TLS* admired the style but found the novel lacking in substance. The *TLS* critic who reviewed a translation of the novel in 1955 went further, considering it a 'brilliant piece of writing but a vile story'.[15]

Though the love triangle is not an uncommon plot in the novel, this one certainly upsets expectations in that one protagonist is non-human. Alain, in his early twenties, is engaged to the 19-year-old

[11] In Colette, *Œuvres*, iii. 1629; my translation.

[12] Colette, *The Vagabond*, 23.

[13] In Colette, *Œuvres*, iii. 1640; my translation.

[14] Quoted in Juliana Schiesari, *Polymorphous Domesticities: Pets, Bodies and Desire in Four Modern Writers* (Oakland: University of California Press, 2012), 63.

[15] Quoted in Callender, *Le Blé en herbe* and *La Chatte*, 53.

Camille, but still profoundly attached to the childhood home he shares with his widowed mother, their servants, and Saha, the little cat whose 'perfect face [...] and long-suffering dignity' (p. 17) had enchanted him a year or two earlier at a cat show, and who has been his constant companion ever since. Alain and Camille duly marry, but Alain's most heartfelt allegiance is to Saha who embodies all the qualities he most values. Camille's jealousy drives the plot to a confrontation in which Camille comes close to killing the cat, and Alain leaves the marriage.

The novel is brilliantly realized through a series of contrasts— contrasts of places, of bodies, and through these of very different views of life and how it should be lived. Though both Alain Amparat and Camille Malmert come from affluent bourgeois families—they used to play together as children—they belong to significantly different layers of the middle class. Alain's family have made their money in the silk trade, once profitable but now losing ground to more modern materials. Their house and garden date from an earlier, more prosperous era in the family fortunes: the house is venerable rather than smart, and is surrounded by a mature garden lyrically described as a lush, flower-filled Eden of spreading trees and deep, soft lawns. Camille's family, on the other hand, manufacture washing machines; they are 'new' money, and Camille disdains as 'a real museum' (p. 36) the outmoded style of Alain's house, with its comfortable but wellworn furnishings and ageing domestic staff. Camille looks forward to the completion of the new, modern extension to the house that is being built to become the newly-weds' home, while Alain loaths its intrusion into the peace of the garden.

The contrast between Alain and Camille then is materialized in the couple's divergent taste in housing, accentuated when the wedding takes place and they move temporarily into an ultra-modern city appartment in a nine-storey block, borrowed from a friend. Camille loves the bright shiny surfaces, the triangular rooms with their huge windows that mean constant exposure to the outside world, the sounds of surrounding construction, and the strains of jazz music that float up from neighbouring flats and gardens. But to Alain this urban world is harshly alien, gratingly metallic and discordant, the antithesis of his beloved garden. The contrast carries through to the protagonists' bodies: Alain's blond, languid grace is at total variance with Camille's dark, agile sensuality, short hair, and physical confidence that Alain soon finds offensive ('What a nerve!' he thinks on the morning after their first night together: 'Stark naked? Where does she think she is?'). Married life makes Alain lose weight, whereas he perceives Camille as feeding off him and growing plump on love: 'She's put on weight because we make love...because of me' (p. 50).

Colette's counter-normative representation of gender difference is central to *La Chatte*. Camille is robust, pragmatic, frank in her desires, competent to navigate the modern world as her skilful driving of the couple's red sportscar suggests, whereas Alain displays the more traditionally 'feminine' qualities of narcissism, passivity, reticence, a preference for familiar domestic spaces. He does not know how to manage the company his father left him, and is patronized and marginalized by his own employees when he attends the office. Camille, on the other hand, although such a possibility is never raised, seems to have all the attributes of a successful businesswoman. In Colette's world it is men who hold the economic, legal, and physical power—as does Alain—but women who are the effective managers, the survivors, adapters, make-do-and-menders, perhaps because they have to be. 'She's already organizing things, putting out feelers, building bridges, pulling things together, mending, picking up the threads again' (p. 83), thinks Alain after their separation. 'A woman can never die of grief', reflects Renée, one of Colette's alter egos, in *The Vagabond*. 'She is such a solid creature, so hard to kill! [...] she gains from grief indestructible nerves, an inflexible pride, a capacity for waiting and dissimulating that increases her stature.'[16] Colette's male protagonists reflect the reality of men's greater social and even physical power, but are represented as the more fragile sex, emotionally and psychologically.

What is both skilled and moving about *The Cat*, though, is the empathetic portrayal of each of the two contrasting characters and through them of opposing attitudes to life. Focalization is almost solely through Alain's eyes, indeed Alain's reflections form the main discourse of the novel, and it is from his perspective that the reader sees Camille as coarse, overbearing, superficial, and materialist, riding roughshod over Alain's feelings. And yet Camille resembles Colette's positive women characters—Léa in *Chéri*, Irène the 'masked woman' in her Pierrot costume, Vinca in *The Ripening Seed* who, like

[16] Colette, *The Vagabond*, 27.

Camille, shocks her lover by her complete lack of shame or embarrassment after they first make love. Camille shares their confident sensuality, their resilience and robust self-respect, maintained even as Alain rejects her, and there is something admirable in her embrace of modernity, her rejection of the sexual reticence expected of young women, her energy. Conversely, Alain's love for the cat—who embodies a delicate, sensitive sensuality, emotional discretion, the scent and texture of the Edenic garden—is persuasively written, and it is not hard to identify with his helpless desire for escape from the inexorable march of time, and all the demands of adulthood, through a return to his childhood home. The garden and the cat are so eloquently drawn that it would be hard to read the novel without feeling sympathy for Alain's love for them.

Yet when he abandons Camille and their future so easily to retreat into the past, the final, distanced view of him dressed in outgrown pyjamas, alone in the garden with Saha, is from Camille's perspective, and narrative sympathy is much less apparent. Of the two, Saha appears the more human. If the yearning for the carefree, nurturing, sensorily rich world of childhood echoes Colette's own depiction of Sido's house and garden, in for example *Claudine's House* (1922), and is treated with understanding, Alain is nonetheless a man who recoils from female sexuality and refuses to see the need to 'build bridges, pull things together, mend, pick up the threads' if life is to go on. The final image condenses Alain's incapacity to move beyond childhood dreams and to deal with the hard reality, but also the potential joys, of a changing world.

For some readers sympathy for Alain will be reinforced too by his inability or unwillingness to live up to the role demanded of him as a middle-class man. Like Chéri, particularly in the 1926 *The End of Chéri*, Alain is in some senses a casualty of the patriarchal system. Lacking authority or commercial instincts, lacking too the capacity and will to manage his future and that of a wife, he fails as an adult male. It is Camille who has all the attributes that this role would require, but as a woman her destiny lies only in the domestic sphere. The reversal of traditionally gendered qualities in the couple implicitly underlines the inadequacy of a strictly binary, prescriptive model of gender, and this reinforces the novel's dual understanding of the two opposed characters and philosophies. In the end, however, Alain's retreat from the present and the future is not condoned. Camille's

final accusation 'C'est *toi* le monstre'—'*You're* the monster' (p. 81)—
has the ring of truth.

The novel, though, is named for the third protagonist, the cat. Cats
had been part of Colette's life since her childhood days in Saint-
Sauveur, for Sido's house was also home to generations of cats,
lovingly evoked in (among other texts) *My Mother's House*. Colette
cherished the company of both cats and dogs, appreciating the
warmth and loyal devotion of the latter as well as the dignified
reserve and independence of cats. Some of her earliest writings
pitched these contrasting attitudes to life against each other in dialogues between the docile, commonsensical dog Toby-chien and the
arrogant but perceptive cat, Kiki-la-Doucette, and many more animal
protagonists would follow, most famously of all in *The Cat*. Though
many animal species are vividly (and empathetically) brought to life
in her work, Colette is most closely associated with cats, and was often
photographed with one of her beloved feline companions, her own
triangular face and almond-shaped eyes creating a physical resemblance with a creature whose characteristic qualities of discretion,
self-sufficiency, and capacity for richly enjoyed sensual pleasure made it
a fitting alter ego for Colette herself. Her writing consistently assumes—
against the dominant Western belief in human exceptionalism—the
interrelatedness of all human and non-human species, but her strong-
est affinity is with cats.

Saha exemplifies Colette's sense of continuity between humans
and other living organisms. She is fully a character in her own right,
realized in sensory terms, with her soft silver-grey fur, her cold little
nose and delicate paws, her quicksilver movements, and through her
body, voice, and gestures we perceive, too, feline emotions and psychology. Saha embodies the dignified freedom that Colette attributes to
animals who have escaped complete subjugation to humans (like the
little fox, still wild beneath his tamed domestication), merging into
the fertile luxuriance of the garden and responding only to the calls
of those she loves. She pines when Alain is absent, adapts determinedly to life in the Quart-de-Brie in order to be with him, whilst
sharing his sense of deprivation, high up above the earth, surrounded
by hard, artificial surfaces. Saha interprets Camille's enmity from her
voice and body language, refuses to show fear but treats her rival with
caution. As the novel ends it is Saha, not Alain, who 'like a human'
watches Camille attentively as she leaves the garden (p. 83). Like the

human protagonists of the novel's triangle, Saha has perceptions, feelings, and agency. But her function in the novel is also to physically embody Alain's most profound desires, or what we might term his child soul. Saha represents the integrity, innocence, and sensory richness of Alain's happy childhood, 'his kingdom', a safe, protected freedom uncompromised by the realities of human society and the passage of time. Camille's attempt to kill Saha is both partially understandable—the cat, incomprehensibly to Camille, blocks the possibility of making a happy life with Alain—and totally unforgivable.

Like most of Colette's writing, the novel works through the senses, by communicating an intensely felt contrast between on the one hand a yearning for a lost, mythical innocence and integrity, and on the other a will to engage fully in a social world of change and compromise. Neither attitude is wholly rejected, for Colette's world view is plural and complex, and acknowledges the co-validity of apparently contradictory values. If *The Cat* proposes any form of morality—and the word is not often used in relation to Colette—then it is this: a sceptical view of embedded, normative categories and values; a respect for otherness that extends beyond the human world; an affirmation of the existential joy of being alive.

The Masked Woman

La Femme cachée—*The Masked Woman*—was published in volume form in 1924. The volume brings together twenty-two short stories, all but one ('Habits') previously published between 1921 and 1923 in the daily *Le Matin*, the newspaper of which Colette was, at the time, literary editor, and whose offices appear in the story 'The Half-Mad'. By this time, as she entered her fifties, Colette had become a well-known and celebrated literary figure in France, especially since the success of her novel *Chéri* in 1920. The 1920s and 1930s were a period of intense creative activity across Colette's many interests and means of making a living: she appeared in touring stage productions of her own novels, playing Renée the 'Vagabond' and Léa, heroine of *Chéri*; she was a prolific journalist, writing for numerous papers and magazines; across the two decades she published some twenty books.

The Masked Woman is composed of brief tales of contemporary life, observed on the whole in domestic or other everyday settings. Each begins in medias res, without preamble ('When Madame de la

Hournerie returned home...' (p. 108), 'When he had killed her...'
(p. 130)), so that we find ourselves immediately inside the fictional
world. Deftly constructed, the stories chart transitional moments in
the lives of their protagonists, in a few cases momentous—two murderers are apprehended by the police, a woman dies—but in most
involving rather a subjective shift, a moment of realization. A husband will never again be able to see in the same light the woman he
thought of as a sweet and docile wife; a happy new bride perceives the
compromise and need for subterfuge her married life will demand;
a divorced woman recognizes that the satisfactions of an affluently
independent life are also shadowed by loneliness and a sense of void.
These are not happy stories, but they offer the pleasures of sharp
observation and of concisely but vividly realized fictional worlds.
Human relations are portrayed as difficult, often painful, but also
endlessly interesting and redeemed by glimpses of a resilient human
capacity for joy.

Certain recurring themes and tropes connect the otherwise dispar-
ate texts. If many of the stories concern, in one way or another, heterosexual couples, Colette's unconventional take on gender roles is
very apparent in the way that her female protagonists are rarely
mothers, and simply do not see maternity as a significant dimension
of their lives. Only Madame Grey in 'Secrets' is portrayed in a maternal role, and her story concerns her anxiety about whether or not to
warn her daughter of the perils of marriage. The critical depiction of
marriage and marginalization of maternity are especially radical in
the context of post-First World War France, with its pro-natalist
stance intensified by the massive loss of male lives in combat, and
idealization of maternity and family as central to national revival. The
1920s in France were an era of oppressive anti-contraception laws,
and an ideological emphasis on motherhood as the 'symbol of rebirth,
healing, redemption and restoration from the war's moral trauma'.[17]
Political speeches, much of the press, and many works of literature
presented marriage and family as the road to salvation for a nation
menaced by depopulation, feminism, and divorce. In Colette's stories, the state of conjugality is seen not as producing happiness and
stability, but as incompatible with self-fulfilment (what in one story is

---

[17] Mary-Louise Roberts, *Civilization without Sexes: Reconstructing Gender in Post-war
France* (Chicago: University of Chicago Press, 1994), 91.

termed the inner 'certainty of being alive' (p. 97)), or at least demanding a pragmatic acceptance of the need for 'duplicity, resignation,
shameful, subtle diplomacy' (p. 100) if the relationship is to survive.
If this is mainly seen from the perspective of female protagonists, it
can also be true for men, like the husband in 'Châ', subjugated by his
'steely and radiant' wife (p. 148). Colette's men, though, are more
likely to react by spontaneous violence than by resigned compromise:
three of the stories involve murders of women by angry men, so that
behind the women's accommodation with the everyday disappointments of conjugality lurks a sense of unequal power and the threats
that this poses. It is the women in these stories who conceal their
desires and displeasures behind a mask of compliance.

Several stories deal with the way in which an individual's sense
of identity depends on the confirmation of another's perception.
Monsieur Maurice, a successful politician, chooses for his secretary
not the well-qualified, visually appealing young candidate but the
older woman who remembers him as a dashing younger man, and can
return to him that sense of his own youthful glamour. Women depend
on the male gaze to affirm their sense of self: a 50-year-old woman
changes her hairstyle for something more fashionable and resists her
own doubts about this new version of herself until she sees the disapproval in the eyes of her butler; 'Game of Mirrors' shows how two
women compete to perform for their male observer, imitating each
other's more successful strategies. The masks that women wear serve
mainly to reassure, flatter, and disarm the men on whom they depend,
often materially but also for confirmation of their own worth in the
eyes of the more powerful sex. The reality of male dominance, and of
the difficulty of living outside its rules, is quietly evident in Colette's
fiction.

Yet female resistance is also a strongly recurring theme, and with it
an affirmation of women's solidarity rather than rivalry. The female
narrator of 'One Evening' recognizes, empathetically, the bleak
unhappiness of her host's politely hospitable wife, in the latter's
strained smile that fails to reach her eyes; Alice reads in the demean-
our of her husband's ex-wife—her smoking, her relaxed leaning back
in her chair—not the surrender of a vanquished rival but the model
of a perhaps more desirable single life. Most clearly of all, in 'The
Portrait' two friends who have loved and been rejected by the same
man emerge from his compelling gaze, and the shrunken sense of

their own lives this induced, to rediscover their lost joie de vivre and a complicit lust for life. 'Their burning desire to escape, full of wicked plans, gave rise to a great deal of eating and drinking, smoking and loose talk' (p. 136). Renewed vitality is shared and takes the very physical form of hunger and thirst, desire to smoke and talk to each other for the sheer pleasure of speaking.

Solidarity is expressed through attention to bodily signs and through shared physical appetites, and in these stories—as elsewhere in Colette—psychology and emotion are registered largely through bodies and the material world. Irène, the 'masked woman', makes no speeches, nor do we see inside her head. Her utter negation of the rules of female respectability is wholly expressed through the flamboyant androgyny of her costume and body language, her coolly predatory enjoyment of both male and female bodies, and the scandalized reaction of the story's focalizer, her husband. The young bride in 'The Hand' recoils not from anything her husband says or does—he is asleep throughout most of the narrative—but from all that is signified by the powerful bestiality of his hand. The murderer in 'The Omelette' does not come to a conscious decision to give himself up rather than remain on the run, but accedes to an intense desire for food and drink, the immediacy of hunger overpowering any concern for safety. In 'The Bracelet', Madame Angelier's desire to recover the intensity of childhood imagination and sense of life's limitless possibilities is embodied in the memory of, and search for, a blue glass bracelet. Dramas play out less through words or verbalized trains of thought than through sense impressions and appetites, and physical encounters. Throughout these stories, Colette's fictional universe is vividly materialized.

The stories are connected too by an element of surprise, of unexpected combinations that defy commonsensical logic. One standard convention of the short story form is the 'twist in the tail', the narrative that ends with a sudden reversal or shock. Maupassant, one of the most celebrated French practitioners of the short story form with whose work Colette would certainly have been familiar, often used this narrative device. Colette's 'twists' are rarely dramatic, but work to challenge received wisdom and generalizations, or, as another critic puts it, to 'dismantle socially constructed categories'.[18] Thus in the

---

[18] Dana Strand, *Colette: A Study of the Shorter Fiction* (New York: Twayne Publishers, 1995), 7.

first story, the husband finds himself almost hoping to discover that his wife is meeting a lover, for mere adultery would be normal and recognizable, unlike the wild freedoms suggested by Irene's behaviour. Paradoxically too, it is the literal mask Irene wears that allows her to abandon her everyday mask of conventional femininity: the mask reveals rather than conceals, and the story ends on the neat oxymoron of her 'deceitful innocence' (p. 90). The burglar in the story of that name behaves not with the callous self-interest the word evokes, but as a 'noble and romantic hero' (p. 125), renouncing a lucrative theft of jewels rather than appear ungentlemanly. In 'The Piece of Advice', an elderly man's cosily avuncular counsel to a young stranger leads not to a restoration of family order, as he hoped, but to murder, and in 'The Assassin', the murderer's final apprehension by the police produces in him not distress, but a passionate sense of relief that he compares to the moment when he fell in love. The deceitfully innocent woman, the honourable burglar, the gentle murderer—these apparently paradoxical characterizations question established categories in the same way that Colette's unmaternal, exuberantly desiring women, concealed behind their pragmatic masks of compliant femininity, question the social construction of gender. *The Masked Woman* assembles a group of deftly constructed tales that focus on moments of transition or revelation in otherwise ordinary lives, written in a style that is richly sensory and questioning of normalized definitions of human reality.

TRANSLATOR'S NOTE

COLETTE's powerful novella *La Chatte* is a psychological drama. It is an unusual take on the theme of the eternal triangle: a young married couple, the wife becoming ever more jealous of her husband's cat. Each time I read it, I have to hold my breath at the crisis in this taut narrative, and I have tried to convey that tension, that acute observation and empathy that is so characteristic of Colette. Her extraordinary understanding of both humans and animals (and their interdealings) is as evident in *La Chatte* as it is in the collection of short stories called *La Femme cachée*. I have used the Livre de Poche edition (Librairie Arthème-Fayard et Hachette Littératures, 2004) for my translation of *La Chatte* and the Folio edition (Gallimard, 1951) for my translation of *La Femme cachée*.

I hesitated before deciding on the title of the latter, usually translated as 'The Hidden Woman'. I hope my title 'The Masked Woman', which pertains particularly to the first story in the collection, also conveys the author's wish to show the condition of being a woman, sometimes mysterious, sometimes secret, still often subjugated. These early stories from 1924, only the second publication of Colette under her own name, are informed throughout by her strong feminism. But as a writer, she is not in the least hidden or masked. Her personality, her love of life, shines through all her writing and, though very much a woman of her time, she speaks for women of all ages.

I'd like to thank OUP, my editor Diana Holmes, as well as Paul Gibbard and David Constantine for their careful reading of the translation and their suggestions.

H.C.

SELECT BIBLIOGRAPHY

Works by Colette

Colette, *Œuvres* (Paris: Bibliothèque de la Pléiade, Gallimard, 1986–2001).

Colette, *Creatures Great and Small* (first published in French in different volumes, 1904–16), trans. Enid McLeod (London: Secker and Warburg, 1951).

Colette, *The Vagabond* (first published in French, 1910), trans. Enid McLeod (Harmondsworth: Penguin, 1960).

Colette, *Break of Day* (first published in French, 1928), trans. Enid McLeod (London: The Women's Press, 1979).

Critical Studies

Callender, Margaret, *Le Blé en herbe* and *La Chatte* (Critical Guides to French Texts; London: Grant & Cutler, 1992).

Eisinger, Erica M., and McCarty, Mari (eds.), *Colette, the Woman, the Writer* (Philadelphia: Pennsylvania University Press, 1981).

Holmes, Diana, *Colette* (Women Writers series; Houndmills: Macmillan, 1991).

Holmes, Diana, 'Everyday Adventures, or What Makes Colette a Feminine Writer', in *French Women's Writing 1848–1994* (London: The Athlone Press, 1996), 125–46.

Holmes, Diana, 'Colette: The Middlebrow Modernist', in *Middlebrow Matters: Women's Reading and the Literary Canon in France since the Belle Époque* (Liverpool: Liverpool University Press, 2018), 60–90.

Kristeva, Julia, *Colette* (first published in French in 2002 as the third volume of *Le Génie féminin*), trans. Jane Marie Todd (Columbia: Columbia University Press, 2004).

Lambert, Emmanuelle, *Sidonie Gabrielle Colette* (Paris: Gallimard, 2023) (in French, but accessible and beautifully illustrated with photographs).

Roberts, Mary-Louise, *Civilization without Sexes: Reconstructing Gender in Post-War France* (Chicago: University of Chicago Press, 1994).

Sarde, Michèle, *Colette: A Biography* (New York: William Morrow & Co., 1971).

Schiesari, Juliana, *Polymorphous Domesticities: Pets, Bodies and Desire in Four Modern Writers* (Oakland: University of California Press, 2012).

Tilburg, Patricia, *Colette's Republic: Work, Gender and Popular Culture in France 1871–1914* (New York: Berghahn Books, 2009).

Ward-Jouve, Nicole, *Colette* (Bloomington: Indiana University Press, 1987).

Film Biopic

Colette, directed by Wash Westmoreland, with Keira Knightley, Fiona Shaw, and Dominic West (2018).

Further Reading in Oxford World's Classics

French Decadent Tales, ed. Stephen Romer.

Maupassant, Guy de, *A Day in the City and Other Stories*, trans. and ed. David Coward.

Proust, Marcel, *Swann in Love*, trans. Brian Nelson, ed. Adam Watt.

Woolf, Virginia, *Flush*, ed. Kate Flint.

A CHRONOLOGY OF COLETTE

Some of Colette's works have appeared in English under more than one title; her works are referred to here by their English titles where there is a standard form but in other cases French titles are given, either followed by an English form in parentheses or alone.

1873 (28 January) Sidonie-Gabrielle Colette born in Saint-Sauveur-en-Puisaye, a town of around 1,700 inhabitants in the Yonne, to Jules Joseph Colette (b. 1829), a tax official and retired army officer whose leg had been amputated after the Battle of Melegnano in 1859, and Adèle Eugénie Sidonie Landoy (b. 1835). Colette's mother, known as 'Sido', had a daughter Juliette (b. 1860) and son Achille (b. 1863) by a previous marriage to Jules Robineau-Duclos (1815–65), and a son Léopold (b. 1866) with Jules Colette.

1879 (October) Gabrielle Colette starts attending the local public school in Saint-Sauveur.

1881 Jules Colette forced to sell land as financial situation worsens.

1889 (July) Gabrielle passes her examinations in Auxerre and is awarded her *brevet élémentaire* (school certificate). Visits Paris where she is introduced to journalist and author Henry Gauthier-Villars (b. 1859), known as 'Willy'.

1891 After selling furniture, the Colette family leave Saint-Sauveur to live with Achille in Châtillon-sur-Loing (now known as Châtillon-Coligny), in the Loiret.

1893 (15 May) Gabrielle marries Willy in Châtillon. Moves to Paris where she mixes with writers and artists.

1894 Publishes first articles in newspaper *La Cocarde*. Learns of Willy's infidelity.

1895–6 Writes reminiscences of her schooldays. Willy apparently places manuscript in a desk drawer and forgets about it.

1900 After rediscovering manuscript, Willy shows it to publishers and *Claudine at School* is put out in March by Ollendorff under pen name 'Willy'. Following slow initial sales, friendly reviews help turn it into a huge commercial success. (September) Willy buys country house Monts-Boucons, near Besançon, which Colette will use as a retreat until 1905.

1901 (March) *Claudine in Paris*, by 'Willy'.

1902 (January) Stage adaptation of *Claudine in Paris* opens with actress Polaire in title role. Willy appears in public with Gabrielle and Polaire as Claudine 'twins'. (May) *Claudine en ménage* (Claudine Married), by 'Willy'.

1903 Co-writes music criticism with Willy for *Gil Blas*. (March) *Claudine s'en va* (Claudine and Annie), by 'Willy'.

1904 (March) *Dialogues de bêtes* (Animal Dialogues), by 'Colette Willy', the first book bearing Colette's name. (June) *Minne*, by 'Willy'.

1905 (May) *Les Égarements de Minne*, by 'Willy'. (17 September) Death of father in Châtillon. Colette takes lessons in mimodrama acting from Georges Wague.

1906 (February) First public performance at Théâtre des Maturins as a faun in mimodrama *Le Désir, l'Amour et la Chimère*. Spends summer with Mathilde de Morny (b. 1863), Marquise de Belbeuf, known as 'Missy', at her villa at Crotoy on the Atlantic coast. (November) Colette and Willy separate. She lives part of the time with Missy. (December) They appear on stage together in mimodrama *La Romanichelle* at the Moulin Rouge.

1907 (3 January) Plays a mummy in mimodrama *Rêve d'Égypte* at the Moulin Rouge, provoking a riot when she kisses Missy, who is playing an Egyptologist in male dress. Police close the show. (February) *La Retraite sentimentale* (The Retreat from Love), the final *Claudine* novel, by 'Colette Willy'. (September–October) Willy sells the rights to the *Claudine* and *Minne* novels. (October) Colette plays speaking role in Sacha Guitry's comedy *Le Crin*. (November) Performs in successful mimodrama *La Chair*, notoriously baring her breast. Reprises role in Paris, regional France, Belgium, and Switzerland over next three years.

1908 (9 September) Suicide of her sister Juliette. (November) *Les Vrilles de la vigne* (The Tendrils of the Vine). (November–December) Plays heroine in *Claudine in Paris* in Brussels and Lyons.

1909 (January–March) Performs lead role in her own play *En camarades*. (April–May) Tours with *Claudine in Paris* to thirty-two French towns. (August) Begins writing *The Vagabond*, based on her experiences as an actress. (November) *L'Ingénue libertine*, by 'Colette Willy', a reworking of the two *Minne* novels.

1910 (January) Starts writing for *Paris-Journal*. (April–May) Tours thirty French towns (accompanied by Missy), performing in two plays. (June) Missy buys an estate for Colette, Rozven, near Saint-Coulomb, on the Breton coast. Divorce from Willy finalized. (November) Visits Naples with lover Auguste Hériot (b. 1886), heir to a Parisian department store fortune. *Claudine* operetta opens at the Moulin Rouge. (18 November) *The Vagabond*. (December) Starts writing column for *Le Matin*, a collaboration that will continue until 1924; editor is future husband Henry de Jouvenel.

1911 (January–February) Performs in play *Xantho chez les courtisanes* in Nice and *La Chair* in Paris. (March) Travels to Tunisia; breaks off relationship with Hériot. (May–June) Meets Jouvenel in Paris without Missy's knowledge. (July) Flees Paris for Rozven after threats of violence from Jouvenel's lover Isabelle de Comminges; breaks off relationship with Missy. (October) Moves in with Jouvenel at 57 Rue Cortambert, Paris. (December) Performs in mimodrama *L'Oiseau de nuit*.

1912 (April) Performs to acclaim in pantomime *La Chatte amoureuse*. (25 September) Mother dies at Châtillon; Colette does not attend funeral. (19 December) Marries Jouvenel in Paris.

1913 (March) *Prrou, Poucette et quelques autres* and *L'Envers du music-hall* (Backstage at the Music Hall). (3 July) Gives birth to daughter Colette Renée de Jouvenel (known as 'Bel-Gazou') in Paris. (October) *L'Entrave* (The Shackle), sequel to *The Vagabond*. (31 December) Brother Achille dies in Paris.

1914 (1 August) French army is mobilized; Jouvenel rejoins his regiment. (3 August) Germany declares war on France. (October) Colette works as a night nurse in a military hospital in Paris.

1915 (June–July) Colette travels in Italy as reporter for *Le Matin*.

1916 (April) *La Paix chez les bêtes*. (September) Jouvenel receives a civilian posting and rejoins Colette in Paris.

1917 (April) In Rome, where she attends filming of *The Vagabond*, starring Musidora. (May–July) Cinema critic for *Film*. (December) *Les Heures longues*.

1918 (February–November) Theatre critic for *L'Éclair*. (March) Film version of *The Vagabond* opens in Paris. (June) Jouvenel mentioned in despatches for bravery. (11 November) Armistice signed. (December) *Dans la foule* (In the Crowd), articles from *Le Matin*.

1919 (February) *Mitsou, ou Comment l'esprit vient aux filles* (Mitsou, or How Girls Grow Wise). (June) Begins affair with Léopold Marchand (b. 1891), dramatist and decorated soldier. (August) Starts writing *Chéri* at Rozven. (December) Takes up position as theatre critic for *Le Matin*.

1920 (March) Film *La Flamme cachée* opens, screenplay by Colette. (2 July) *Chéri*. (July–August) Begins affair with stepson Bertrand de

Jouvenel (b. 1903) at Rozven. (25 September) Named *chevalier* of the Legion of Honour.

1921 (January) *La Chambre éclairée*. (February) *Celle qui en revient, suivi de quelques autres dialogues de bêtes*, the first of her books to be published under the name 'Colette'. (December) Stage adaptation of *Chéri* opens and is well received.

1922 (April) *Le Voyage égoïste* (Journey for Myself). (June) *La Maison de Claudine* (Claudine's House).

1923 (February) Stage adaptation of *The Vagabond* opens. (March) *Le Matin* halts serial publication of *Le Blé en herbe* (Green Wheat) due to its perceived immorality. (July) Book publication of *Le Blé en herbe*. (December) Henry de Jouvenel leaves their shared home at 69 Boulevard Suchet and Bertrand de Jouvenel moves in.

1924 (March) *La Femme cachée* (The Masked Woman). (April–October) Writes for *Le Figaro*. (December) Plays Léa in stage adaptation of *Chéri* in Monte Carlo and Marseilles.

1925 Performs in *Chéri* in Paris and regions. (21 March) *L'Enfant et les sortilèges* (The Child and the Magic Spells), opera with libretto by Colette and music by Maurice Ravel, opens in Monte Carlo. (6 April) Divorce from Henry de Jouvenel is finalized. Begins relationship with pearl-dealer and journalist Maurice Goudeket and breaks up with Bertrand de Jouvenel.

1926 (March) *The End of Chéri*. (April–May) Travels with Maurice Goudeket in Morocco. (July) Buys villa near Saint-Tropez which she names 'La Treille muscate' (The Muscat Vine). (November) Moves into cramped mezzanine flat in the Palais-Royal, 9 Rue de Beaujolais, Paris. (November–December) Plays Renée Néré on stage in *The Vagabond*.

1928 (March) *Break of Day*. (5 November) Named *officier* of the Legion of Honour.

1929 (March) *La Seconde* (The Other Woman). (May) *Regarde*, illustrated by Mathurin Méheut. (Novembre) *Sido ou les points cardinaux* (Sido or the Cardinal Points).

1930 (May) Publishes expanded version of *Sido*. (December) Moves into suite at the Hôtel Claridge on the Champs-Élysées, where she will reside for four years.

1931 (12 January) Death of Willy. (May) Talking film version of *The Vagabond* opens, screenplay by Colette.

1932 (January) *Ces plaisirs…* (June) Opens beauty business at 6 Rue du Miromesnil, Paris, with further branches in Saint-Tropez and Nantes. (November) *Prisons et paradis*.

1933 (May) *The Cat.* (October) Appointed theatre critic for *Le Journal.*

1934 (July) *La Jumelle noire* (Black Binoculars), a collection of Colette's theatre criticism. Four further volumes of criticism will appear under this title. (August) Adapts *Backstage at the Music-Hall* for film *Divine*, directed by Max Ophüls. Film *Lac-aux-Dames*, directed by Marc Allégret with dialogue by Colette, opens in Paris. (November) *Duo.*

1935 (February) Moves from Hôtel Claridge to Marignan building, also on the Champs-Élysées. (March) Elected to the Belgian Royal Academy of French Language and Literature. (3 April) Marries Maurice Goudeket in Paris. (May–June) Travels to New York as reporter on maiden voyage of SS *Normandie*. (5 October) Death of Henry de Jouvenel.

1936 (January) *My Apprenticeships.* (March) *Cats*, illustrated by Jacques Nam.

1937 (November) Film version of *Claudine at School* opens. (November) *Bella-Vista.*

1938 (January) Moves into first-floor apartment at 9 Rue de Beaujolais, in the Palais-Royal, where she will reside until death. (June) Moves from *Le Journal* to *Paris-Soir*. (October) Stage adaptation of *Duo* opens. (November) *Paris*, illustrated by Reine Cimière.

1939 (January) *Le Toutounier*, sequel to *Duo*. (3 September) France declares war on Germany. Colette makes live broadcasts with Maurice Goudeket to American listeners on Paris-Mondial radio station, which continue through winter.

1940 (7 March) Death of brother Léopold Colette. (13 June) Drives south during exodus (with Maurice Goudeket and servant Pauline Vérine) to stay with daughter in Curemonte in the Corrèze. (14 June) German army enters Paris. (11 July) Returns to Paris. Writes for *Le Petit Parisien* and will contribute to collaborationist newspapers during the Occupation. (November) *Chambre d'hôtel.*

1941 (April) *Journal à rebours* (Looking Backwards). (July) *Mes cahiers* (My Notebooks). (October) *Julie de Carneilhan*. (November) *Le Pur et l'Impur* (The Pure and the Impure), a reworking of *Ces plaisirs...* (12 December) Maurice Goudeket, who is Jewish, arrested by the Germans and interned in Compiègne; Colette lobbies for his release.

1942 (6 February) Maurice Goudeket released. (May) *De ma fenêtre* (From My Window), collection of articles from *Le Petit Parisien*. Treated for osteoarthritis, which will severely limit her mobility in remaining years; buys a motorized wheelchair.

1943 (March) *Le Képi*. (July) *De la patte à l'aile*, a collection of previously published pieces on animals. (August) *Flore et Pomone*. (November) *Nudité*, illustrated by Carlègle.

1944 (June) *Gigi et autres nouvelles* (Gigi and Other Stories). (29 June) Death of Missy by suicide. (July) *Paris de ma fenêtre* (Paris from My Window). (24 August) Liberation of Paris. (December) *Trois... Six...Neuf...* (Three...Six...Nine...).

1945 (2 May) Elected to Académie Goncourt. (7 May) Germany surrenders. (November) *Belles Saisons*.

1946 (March) *L'Étoile vesper* (The Evening Star).

1948 Publication of Colette's complete works in fifteen volumes by Éditions du Fleuron begins and will be completed in 1950.

1949 (January) *Pour un herbier*. (May) *Le Fanal bleu* (The Blue Lamp). (October) Colette appointed president of the Académie Goncourt. Film version of *Gigi* opens, with Danièle Delorme in title role. Four collections of Colette's journalism published during year: *Trait pour trait*; *Journal intermittent*; *La Fleur de l'âge*; *En pays connu*.

1950 (April–May) Film versions of *Julie de Carneilhan*, *Chéri*, and *Minne* open. (May–July) Stays at Hôtel de Paris in Monte Carlo, where she will return each spring.

1951 (January) Gala opening for stage adaptation of *La Seconde* in Paris. First screening of Yannick Bellon's documentary film *Colette*. (November) Anita Loos's stage adaptation of *Gigi*, with Audrey Hepburn in title role, opens on Broadway.

1953 (3 March) Colette named *grand officier* of the Legion of Honour. (April) *Le Ciel de lit* (The Four-Poster) opens, French adaptation by Colette and Maurice Goudeket of play by Dutch writer Jan de Hartog. (May) US ambassador awards Colette diploma of National Institute of Arts and Letters.

1954 (January) Controversial film version of *Le Blé en herbe* opens. (February) French-language stage adaptation of *Gigi* opens in Paris. (3 August) Death of Colette at home, after slow decline in health. (7 August) State funeral held in courtyard of Palais-Royal; Colette buried in Père-Lachaise Cemetery.

THE CAT

Around ten o'clock, the poker players of the family were showing signs of fatigue. Camille was fighting her tiredness, as you do when you are nineteen, that is, she livened up again in fits and starts; then she would hide a yawn behind her hands and her face and chin would grow pale again, her cheeks slightly darken beneath her gold-tinted powder, and two small tears appear in the corners of her eyes.

'Camille, you should go to bed!'

'At ten o'clock, Maman, ten o'clock! Who on earth goes to bed at ten?'

She looked for support from her fiancé, who had collapsed into a deep armchair.

'Leave them alone,' another maternal voice intervened. 'They've still got another week to wait. They are being rather silly at the moment. It's quite understandable.'

'Exactly, so what's an hour more or less? Camille, you ought to go to bed. And we should too.'

'A week!' exclaimed Camille. 'Oh, that's right, it's Monday! I forgot...Alain, come over here!'

She threw her cigarette out into the garden, lit another, sorted and shuffled the abandoned poker cards and laid them out in a cabbalistic fashion.

'We need to find out if we can have that sweet little baby sports car, before we get married! Look, Alain. I'm not making it up! It says there'll be a journey and an important piece of news...'

'What's that?'

'The sports car of course!'

Alain, not raising his head, turned to look through the open French windows, through which came the sweet fragrance of spinach and new-mown hay, for the grass had been cut during the day. The scent of honey from the first honeysuckle flowers draped over a tall, dead tree also wafted over to them. The clinking of crystal announced the arrival of the ten o'clock fruit syrup and iced water in old Émile's trembling hands, and Camille got up to fill the glasses.

She served her fiancé last, handed him the cloudy tumbler with a conspiratorial smile. As she watched him drink, the sight of his mouth pressing against the rim of the glass suddenly troubled her; but he was feeling so weary he refused to acknowledge her emotion and just squeezed the white fingers and red nails lightly as they took the tumbler from him.

'Are you coming to lunch tomorrow?' she asked him softly.

'Read the cards!'

Camille drew away, and made a funny face, like a clown:

'Never joke about Twenty-four Hours! Joke about crossed knives, if you like, or pennies with holes in, Talking Pictures, or ask the Almighty…

'Camille!'

'Sorry, Maman…but let's not make fun of Twenty-four Hours! He's a good sort, the Jack of Spades, the little dark speedy messenger— always in a hurry…'

'In a hurry to do what?'

'In a hurry to talk of course! Just think about it! He brings the news for the next twenty-four hours, for two days even. If you put two more cards on his right and left, he predicts what will happen the following week…'

She talked quickly, picking at two tiny red smudges of lipstick on the corner of her lips with a sharp fingernail. Alain listened, neither bored nor indulgent. He had known her for several years and in his estimation, she was typical of the modern young woman. He was aware she drove a car rather too fast, rather too confidently, her eyes all over the place, and her bright red lips always ready to mouth obscenities at taxicabs. He knew she could tell lies without blushing, like children and adolescents; that she was capable of deceiving her parents in order to meet Alain after dinner in the clubs where they danced, but where they only drank orange juice because Alain didn't like alcohol.

Before their official engagement, she had offered him in sun and shade her lips carefully wiped, her breasts, impersonal and always encased in two cups of lacy tulle, and her extremely beautiful legs in perfect stockings which she bought on the sly, stockings 'like Mistinguett's,* you know? Be careful of my stockings, Alain!' Her stockings, her legs, they were the best things about her…

'She's pretty,' Alain told himself, 'there's nothing ugly about her, she's a classic brunette, her sparkling eyes match her sleek, glossy hair that she washes all the time, the colour of the black keys on a brand-new piano.' And he was not unaware of the fact that she had a sharp tongue and could be as unpredictable as a mountain stream.

She was still talking about the sports car.

'Oh no, Papa! Of course I wouldn't let Alain drive when we cross Switzerland! He gets too distracted—and when it comes down to it, he doesn't much like driving—I know him!'

'She knows me,' echoed Alain to himself. 'Or perhaps she thinks she does. I have said to her scores of times myself "I know you, my girl!" Saha knows her too. Where is our Saha?' He looked to see if he could see the cat and hoisted himself out of his armchair, first one shoulder and then the other, then his hips and finally his backside, and languidly descended the five steps to the garden.

The garden was huge, surrounded by other gardens, and at night gave off the rich scent of well-tended flower beds, regularly encouraged to grow and flourish. The house had changed little since Alain was born. 'The house of an only child,' thought Camille, who didn't disguise her contempt for the steep-pitched roof, the windows at the top set in under the slates, and for some of the modest mouldings around the sides of the French windows on the ground floor.

Like Camille, the garden seemed to gaze disdainfully at the house. Very tall elms, raining the chalky black twigs that such trees shed in their old age, shielded it from the neighbours and passers-by. A little further down on a plot for sale in the yard of a secondary school, you could see, in stray pairs, the same old elms, survivors of a princely four-lane avenue, all that remained of a park ravaged by the expansion of buildings in Neuilly.*

'Where are you, Alain?'

Camille shouted from the top of the steps, but on a whim, instead of answering, he moved further into the seclusion of the shadows, feeling for the edge of the mown lawn with his foot. High in the sky sat a veiled moon, enlarged by the mist of the first warm days. One solitary tree, a poplar with smooth young leaves, captured the bright moonshine and dripped as many gleams as a cascade of water. A streak of quicksilver leapt out of a flower bed and slithered like a fish against Alain's legs.

'Ah there you are, Saha! I was looking for you. Why didn't you come in to eat this evening?'

'Mer-aaow,' the cat replied, 'Mer-aaow.'

'Mer-aaow? Why mer-aaow? What sort of answer is that?'

'Mer-aaow,' the cat insisted.

With his hand he tenderly explored the long spine that was softer than rabbit fur, then felt the small wet nostrils, dilated by her pulsating purr. 'My little cat…my own little cat.'

'Mer-aaow,' the cat mewed softly. 'R-aaow…'

There was another call from Camille in the house and Saha disappeared beneath a trimmed euonymus hedge, black-green as the night.

'Alain! We're going!'

He started to run towards the steps, and was met by a smiling Camille.

'Look at your hair when you run like that,' she cried. 'It's crazy you being so blond as you are.'

He ran faster, took the five steps with a leap and found Camille alone in the drawing room.

'Where are the others?' he asked under his breath.

'In the hall,' she said equally quietly. 'In the hall and looking at the "building works". Universal despair. "There's no progress! It'll never be finished!" Well, we don't give a fig! If we had our wits about us, we'd keep Patrick's apartment for us, and Patrick could get another. I'll see about it, shall I?'

'But Patrick will only leave the Quart-de-Brie* to be nice to you…'

'Well yes! One should make the most of it.'

She radiated immorality in that manner peculiar to women, which Alain couldn't get used to. But he objected only to her saying 'one' instead of 'we' and she thought it was a fond reproach.

'I'll soon get into the habit of saying "we".'

To make him kiss her she playfully switched off the main light. The only lamp left, on the table, projected a clear, long shadow behind the young woman.

Camille, with her arms raised and hands joined in a curve at the back of her neck, gave him an inviting look. But he only wanted to look at the shadow. 'It's so beautiful on the wall! Just elongated enough, just as I'd want…'

He sat down to compare the one with the other. Flattered, Camille arched her back, thrust out her breasts, and executed an arabesque, but her shadow could do it better than she did. Unclasping her hands, the young woman began to walk, preceded by the exemplary shadow. Once arrived at the open door, the shadow jumped aside and fled into the garden, on to the pink gravel path, embracing the poplar covered

with moon drops as it went…'What a pity…' Alain sighed. He felt
rather sorry then about his tendency to love an idealized or static
form of Camille, like this shadow, for example, her portrait, or the
vivid memory she left of certain occasions, certain dresses…

'What's the matter with you this evening? At least come and help
me on with my cape…'

He was shocked by the insinuation of that 'At least', and also by
Camille's imperceptible shrug as she passed in front of him through
the door that led to the hall and the kitchen. 'She doesn't need to
shrug her shoulders. Nature and habit are doing that for her anyway.
When she doesn't pay attention, her neck makes her look dumpy, ever
so slightly dumpy.'

In the hall they met Alain's mother and Camille's parents who,
stamping their feet as though trying to keep warm on the mat, left
footprints the colour of dirty snow. The cat, sitting outside on the
windowsill, was watching them coldly, but without animosity. Alain
copied its patient attitude as he endured the ritual demonstrations of
pessimism.

'No change then…'

'There's been no progress for a week.'

'If you want to know how I feel about it, my dear, it'll not be a fortnight, it'll be a month—what am I saying, a month?—two months
before their little nest…'

At the word 'nest', Camille threw herself into the peaceful fray, so
sharply that Alain and Saha closed their eyes.

'But we've said what we want! And, actually, we'd enjoy living in
Patrick's rooms! And that would be very good for Patrick too because
he is broke—sorry, Maman, he hasn't any money…We pack our bags
and hey presto, we are sky-high on the ninth floor. Isn't that right,
Alain?'

He opened his eyes again, smiled vaguely and placed the brightly
coloured cape around her shoulders. In the mirror opposite he registered Camille's dark look of reproach, but it didn't increase his
remorse. 'I didn't kiss her properly when we were on our own. Well
no, I didn't kiss her on that mouth of hers. She hasn't had her quota
of proper kisses today! She had the one at a quarter to twelve in an
avenue in the Bois, the one at two o'clock after coffee, the one at six-
thirty in the garden, but she's missed out on this evening's kiss. Well,
let her put it on her account if she's not happy. What's wrong with

me? I'm dog-tired. It's a stupid life we're leading. Things are not good when we see each other and we see each other much too much. On Monday I shall simply go to the shop and...'

In his imagination the acid, chemical smell of the pieces of new silk reached his nostrils. But the impenetrable smile of Monsieur Veuillet appeared, and as in a dream, he heard him say the words which he had not yet learned, aged twenty-four, not to fear. 'No, no, my young friend, a new accounting machine costing seventeen thousand francs, will it pay off the outlay within a year? That's the point. Allow your poor father's oldest associate...' And seeing in the mirror the beautiful black eyes vindictively spying on him, he put his arms around Camille.

'Well, Alain?'

'Oh my dear girl, let him be! These poor children...!'

Camille blushed and freed herself, then held out her cheek to Alain with such boyish, fraternal grace that he almost took refuge on her shoulder. 'To go to bed, to sleep...Oh goodness, to go to bed, to sleep...'

From the garden came the cat's voice:

'Mer-aaow! Raaow!'

'Listen to that cat! She must be hunting,' Camille said calmly. 'Saha! Saha!'

The cat was silent.

'Hunting?' Alain demurred. 'What do you mean? In the first place it's May. And secondly, she is saying "Mer-aaow!"'

'So what?'

'She wouldn't say "mer-aaow" if she were hunting. What she's saying—and it's somewhat odd, mind you—is a warning, almost like a cry to gather her kittens round her.'

'Oh my Lord!' Camille exclaimed, throwing up her arms. 'If Alain starts interpreting what the cat's saying, there'll be no end of it!'

She jumped down the steps into the garden where, beneath the trembling hand of old Émile, two huge old-fashioned purple globes lit up.

Alain walked ahead with Camille. At the gate he kissed her under her ear, breathed in the good smell of bread and dark fur from beneath a perfume which made her seem older than she was, and squeezed the bare elbows of the young woman under her cape. When she took her seat at the wheel, with her parents in the back, he felt alive and cheerful.

'Saha! Saha!'

The cat shot out of the shadows almost beneath his feet, ran when he ran, in great leaps in front of him. He guessed where she was before he saw her, she erupted into the hall in front of him and came back to wait at the top of the steps. With her throat puffed out and her ears down, she watched him run up to her, provoking him with her yellow eyes, deep-set, suspicious, proud, completely confident.

'Saha! Saha!'

Spoken aloud in that special way, softly, with the 'h' strongly aspirated, her name sent her crazy. She waved her tail, bounded on to the poker table and, with her two cat's paws open wide, scattered the playing cards in all directions.

'That cat, that cat...' came his mother's voice. 'She's got no notion of how to behave towards guests. Look how delighted she is to see our friends leave!'

Alain chuckled childishly, as he was wont to do in extreme privacy at home but never outside the confines of the elm-tree path or the black front gate. Then he let out a desperate yawn.

'Good Lord, how tired you look! How can you possibly look so tired when you are happy? There's some orangeade left. No? So, we can go to bed. Leave it, Émile will put the lights out.

'Maman talks to me as though I was just recovering from illness or as if I was going down again with some kind of typhoid infection.'

'Saha, Saha! Oh that wretched cat! Alain, can't you make that cat...'

By climbing vertically up a familiar line on the threadbare brocatelle,* the cat had almost managed to reach the ceiling. For a moment she looked like a grey lizard flattened against the wall with her paws splayed, then she feigned dizziness and uttered an affected little mew. Alain went and stood below her, offering her his shoulders, and Saha came down, stuck to the wall like a raindrop falling slowly down a windowpane. She put her paws on Alain's shoulders and they went up to their bedroom together.

A long black cluster of laburnum hanging outside the open window became pale yellow when Alain lit the ceiling light and his bedside lamp. He bent his shoulder and tipped the cat on to the bed, wandering aimlessly from bedroom to bathroom like a man prevented through fatigue from going to bed.

He leaned out into the garden, surveying the piles of white unfinished building work with some hostility, then opened and closed the drawers and boxes which concealed his real secrets: a gold dollar, an engraved ring, an agate hanging on his father's watch chain; a few red and black seeds from an exotic paradise flower; a mother-of-pearl string of beads from a first communion; a fragile broken bracelet, souvenir of a tempestuous affair with a young mistress who had arrived and vanished in the twinkling of an eye, creating a lot of fuss...The rest of his earthly goods just consisted of books, bound and unbound, letters, photographs...

He handled these pieces of flotsam as if in a dream, they were shiny and of no value, like the coloured stones you find in the nests of thieving birds. 'Should I throw all this away or leave it here? I don't care about it...Do I care about it?' His status of only child meant that he was attached to everything he had never had to share or quarrel over.

He caught sight of his face in the mirror and got annoyed with himself. 'Oh, go to bed for heaven's sake! You're a wreck, you should be ashamed,' he said to the handsome blond young man. 'People only say I'm handsome because I'm blond. If I had dark hair, I'd be frightful.' He looked critically once more at his somewhat equine nose, his long cheeks. But once more he smiled, displaying his teeth, stroked his thick blond hair and admired the subtle shade of his eyes between his dark lashes, a grey verging on green. Two folds hollowed his cheeks on either side of his smile, the eyes receded, surrounded by mauve. A rough pale stubble only that morning shaved clean was already adding volume to his lips. 'What an ugly mug! I am pitiful. No, I disgust myself. Is that the sort of face for a wedding night?' In the mirror Saha was staring at him from far off, with a grave expression.

'I'm coming! I'm coming!'

He threw himself down on the fresh sheets, leaving space for the cat. He addressed to her some ritual litanies appropriate to the grace and virtues of a pure race Chartreux,* small but perfect.

'My fat-cheeked teddy-bear...My little beauty...My dove...My pearl-grey demon...'

As soon as he put out the light, the cat began to gently knead her friend's chest, piercing his silk pyjamas with one claw only each time and touching the skin just enough for Alain to endure a nervous pleasure.

'Another seven days, Saha,' he sighed.

In seven days, seven nights, a new life in a new home with a loving and incorrigible young wife. He stroked the cat's fur, warm and cool, smelling of pruned box, cedar, and well-tended lawns. She was purring loudly, and, in the darkness, she gave him a feline kiss, placing her wet nose for a moment under Alain's, between the nostrils and lips—a fleeting, ethereal kiss which she only bestowed on rare occasions.

'Oh Saha, our nights together...'

The headlights of a car from the nearest avenue pierced the leaves in two white revolving beams. On the bedroom wall the shadows of the laburnum and of the tulip tree in the middle of the lawn grew longer. Above his own face Alain could see Saha's lighten, then darken again as she lay there with a serious look on her face.

'Don't scare me!' he begged.

Nearly asleep, he was weakening again, insubstantial, held fast in the web of an interminable, sweet adolescence.

He shut his eyes while Saha, keeping watch, followed the signs and wonders that dance around those who are asleep, once the light is out.

His dreams were abundant, and he sank into them by degrees. When he woke he told no one about his night's adventures, being secretive about a part of his life which had gone on somewhat longer than usual because of his delicate, ill-managed childhood, and periods in bed during his sudden spurts of growth as a lanky and never very robust adolescent.

He liked his dreams and cultivated them, and nothing in the world would have made him reveal the stages that he went through on the way. At the first stage, while still hearing the car horns on the avenue, he could see faces going round in circles, elongated, familiar, shapeless, and these he passed through with the occasional greeting, as he might have passed through a benign crowd. Round and round they went, convex, increasing in size as they approached. Bright on a dark background, they grew brighter, as though they received light from the sleeper himself. Each with a single bulging eye, they moved in easy gyrations. But touching some invisible barrier, they were flung back in a sudden underwater volte-face in the moist gaze of a round monster, in the iris of a plump moon or in that of a lost archangel whose hair was rays of light, and Alain recognized the same expression, the same intention, which none of them had yet disclosed but which Alain, the dreamer, understood with certainty to mean: 'They will tell me tomorrow.'

Sometimes they exploded into small fragments, scattering into distant shards of light. At other times they existed only as a hand, an arm, a forehead, an optical globe full of thoughts, an astral dust of nose, chins, but without fail as that rounded eye which at the very moment when it might have elucidated things turned and showed only its other, dark side.

Asleep, under Saha's protection, Alain followed his nightly shipwreck, went beyond the world, and descended through eyes and convex faces, a dark zone which allowed no other colour than an intense black, but was itself inexpressibly various and composed of colours that were as if submerged in water, and there on the borders he found his footing in a complete dream now come to fruition.

He collided with a barrier and there was a loud noise, like the clanging of reverberating cymbals. And he emerged into the city of dreams amongst the passers-by, where householders in their doorways, wardens of squares with gold crowns on their heads, and other minor characters were standing along Alain's route as he went by, stark naked, armed with a slender walking stick, extremely lucid and knowing: 'If I walk quite fast after I've knotted my tie in that special way and especially if I whistle, there's a good chance nobody will notice I'm completely naked.' So he knotted his tie in the shape of a heart and whistled. 'What I am doing now isn't whistling, it's snoring. Whistling is like this...' But he went on snoring. 'I am not at my wits' end yet, all I have to do, quite simply, is get past this square flooded with sunlight, walk round the kiosk where the military music is playing. It's child's play. I take off, making dangerous jumps to distract people's attention, and land in the zone of shadows.'

But he felt paralysed by the warm and dangerous look of a swarthy character with a Greek profile, through which showed the large eye of a carp. 'The zone of shadows, the zone of shadows...' Two long shadowy arms, graceful and fluttering with poplar leaves, hurried by at the word 'shadow' and carried Alain off to sleep, during the most ambiguous hour of the short night in that temporary tomb where the living exile sighs, soaks himself in tears, struggles and succumbs, and is reborn, remembering nothing, when daylight comes.

2

THE sun was high in the sky and had reached the windowsill when Alain woke. The cluster of laburnum just coming into flower was translucid, hanging above Saha's head, a daytime Saha, blue and innocent, busy washing herself.

'Saha!'

'Mer-aaow!' replied the cat emphatically.

'Is it my fault if you're hungry? All you had to do was go down and ask for your milk if you're in a hurry.'

She calmed down at the sound of her friend's voice and repeated the same word but this time more quietly, exposing her pink mouth with its row of white teeth. At her look, full of a loyal and exclusive devotion, Alain was alarmed: 'Oh goodness, this cat...What am I to do with her? I'd forgotten I'm getting married. And that I've got to stay at Patrick's...'

He turned to look at the portrait in the chrome-plated frame where Camille was shining, as though bathed in oil, a great pool of reflected light on her hair, her vitrified enamel mouth black as ink, her huge eyes looking out through the palisades of her eyelashes.

'A fine, professional job,' Alain muttered.

He'd forgotten he had himself chosen to hang in his bedroom a photograph that was nothing like Camille, nor anyone else for that matter. 'That eye...I saw that eye...' He took a pencil and slightly reduced the eye, thinned out the excess white and only succeeded in spoiling the print.

'Mouek mouek mouek...m-a-a-a...m-a-a-a,' Saha said, talking to a small silk moth imprisoned between the glass and the net curtain.

Her leonine chin quivered, she was stuttering with desire. Alain captured the moth between two fingers to give it to the cat.

'Hors d'œuvre, Saha!'

Someone was casually combing the gravel path with a rake. Alain could well imagine the hand guiding the rake, the hand of an ageing woman, mechanically, but gently, insistent in its large, white glove like a gendarme's...

'Good morning, Maman!' he shouted.

There was a distant answering voice, a voice whose words he did not hear, an affectionate murmur, meaningless but necessary. He ran down, with the cat at his heels. When it was properly light, she changed into a kind of unruly dog, skittering down the stairs, emerging into the garden with inelegant leaps, quite devoid of magic. She sat on the small breakfast table in the patch of sunlight next to Alain's place. The rake, which had fallen silent, now slowly resumed its work.

Alain poured Saha's milk, mixed with a pinch of salt and a pinch of sugar, and then gravely poured his own. When breakfasting alone, he didn't have to feel embarrassed about some of the things he did, habits he had unconsciously bound himself to between his fourth year and his seventh, the age of obsessions. He could blind all the 'eyes' in his bread with butter as much as he liked, and frown when his coffee rose higher than the level marked by a particular gold arabesque on the inside of his cup. A second thin piece of buttered bread had to follow the first thick one, while the second cup needed an extra sugar cube. In short, the small boy, Alain, concealed beneath the tall, fair, handsome young man, was waiting impatiently for breakfast to be over and allow him to lick the honey spoon clean, an old spoon in blackened and cartilaginous ivory.

'At this moment Camille is eating her breakfast standing up and walking around. She is biting into a thin sliver of ham sandwiched between two *biscottes*,* and along with it an American apple. And as she moves from one piece of furniture to the next, she'll put her cup of tea without sugar down and forget all about it.'

He looked up at his domain, the domain of a privileged upbringing which he cherished and felt he knew intimately. Above his head only the tips of the young leaves on the old elms, cut back hard along the paths, were quivering slightly. Swathes of pink campion, edged with forget-me-nots, had pride of place on a lawn. From the emaciated branch of a dead tree there hung a mantilla of polygonum tangled up with purple, four-petalled clematis, moving gently with each passing breath of air. One of those garden sprinklers standing on its one leg was revolving on the lawn, opening out its white peacock tail striped with a tremulous rainbow.

'What a beautiful garden...So beautiful,' murmured Alain. He noted with disgust the piles of rubbish, planks, and bags of plaster which disgraced the west side of the house. 'Oh, it's Sunday so they're not working. Every day's Sunday for me...' Although he was young and given to moods, as well as somewhat spoilt, he lived according to the commercial rhythm of the week and *sensed* that it was Sunday.

A furtive white pigeon moved behind the weigelas and pinkish deutzia flowers. 'Ah, it's not a pigeon, it's Maman's hand with a glove on.' The big white glove close to the ground was lifting a stem, pinching out weeds that had sprung up overnight. Two greenfinches on the gravel path came to peck at the crumbs from breakfast and Saha observed them impassively. But a blue tit hanging upside down from an elm tree above the table chirped defiantly at the cat. Sitting with her paws together, her beautiful female frill tensed and her head back, Saha was trying to control herself but her cheeks swelled in anger and her small nostrils were damp.

'As beautiful as a she-devil! More beautiful!' Alain said.

He tried to stroke her wide forehead, which was harbouring such fierce thoughts, and suddenly the cat bit him to vent her anger. He looked at the two little specks of blood on the palm of his hand with the anger of a man bitten by his woman in the throes of passion.

'You bad girl...Look what you've done to me!'

She bent her head down, sniffed the blood, and looked timidly at her friend's face. She knew how to distract him, bring him round, and she picked up a *biscotte* from the place mat and held it between her paws like a squirrel.

The May breeze passed over them, and a yellow rosebush that smelled of gorse bent slightly. Between the cat, the rosebush, the pairs of bluetits and the last maybugs, Alain relished the moments of escape from the human span, and felt again the anxious illusion of wandering into his childhood. The elms were immeasurably tall, the broad avenue was lost beneath the poles of a defunct trellis and, like the haunted sleeper who falls off a tower, Alain suddenly remembered that he was twenty-four years old.

'I should have slept another hour. It's only half past nine. It's Sunday. It was Sunday for me yesterday too. Too many Sundays...But tomorrow...'

Then, with a complicit smile at Saha: 'Tomorrow, Saha, it's the final trying-on of the white dress. I shan't be there. It's to be a surprise...Camille is dark enough for the white to show off her beauty. While they are doing that, I'll take a look at the car. It's a two-seater, a bit cheap, a bit inferior, as Camille says. That's what you get from being married so young.'

The cat executed a vertical leap, rising like a fish to the water's surface, and caught a small white, black-edged butterfly. She ate it, coughed, spat out a wing, and licked herself ostentatiously. The sun played on her Chartreux fur, mauve with touches of blue like the throats of wood pigeons.

'Saha!'

She looked round and smiled steadily at him.

'My little puma! My darling cat! My mountain lion! How will you go on living if we leave each other? Shall we both take Orders? Shall we...Oh, I don't know...'

She listened, looked at him lovingly and unconcernedly, but when his voice grew more emotional, looked away again.

'Well, in the first place, you'll be coming with us. You don't mind the car. If we have the cabriolet and not the sports car, there's a ledge behind the seats...'

He stopped and darkened at the recent memory of a girl's voice, which she could raise to a shout when she liked, enunciating the main vowels 'a' and 'o', capable of reciting the numerous advantages of the sports car. 'And then when you put the windscreen down, Alain, it's tremendous, at full throttle you can feel the skin on your cheeks, it almost flattens them against your ears.'

'Against your ears, Saha, just think of that! Horrific!'

He pursed his lips, made a long face like a stubborn child, who knows how to get his own way by guile.

'It's not decided yet. Supposing I prefer the cabriolet? After all, I imagine I have some say in the matter?'

He looked scornfully at the yellow rosebush as though it were the girl with the beautiful voice. Once again, the garden path widened, the elms grew tall, the trellis leafed. From behind the skirts of two or three rather lofty aunts whose heads seemed to touch the sky, the child Alain peeped out at another family group which included a little dark-haired girl, with big jet-black eyes and ringlets, both equally disconcerting in their cold hostility. 'Say hello! Why won't you say hello?' It was a voice from the past, faint, remembered all through the years of childhood, adolescence, school, the boredom in the army, fake seriousness, fake commercial competence. Camille did not want to say hello. She sucked the inside of her cheeks and made a stiff little-girl curtsey. 'Nowadays she calls that a "twisted bob". But when she is angry, she still bites the inside of her cheeks. And curiously enough, it doesn't make her ugly.'

He smiled and grew genuinely aroused at the thought of his fiancée, pleased after all that she had a healthy, if somewhat banal, sensual passion. Faced with the purity of the morning, he conjured up images that now roused his vanity and impatience, now gave rise to apprehension and even dismay. As the emotion subsided, he found the sun too bright and the wind biting. The cat had disappeared, but as soon as Alain got up, she was there beside him and walked along with him with the long stride of a deer, avoiding the round pebbles of the pink gravel path. Together they went to visit the 'works', inspected with equal resentment the heap of rubble, new French windows without any glass in them inserted into a wall, some bathroom appliances, and some pottery tiles.

Equally offended, they both assessed the damage caused to their past and present. An old yew tree, torn out of the earth, was dying a slow death upside down, with its roots above like a head of hair. 'I should never have allowed that, never,' muttered Alain. 'It's shameful. You've only known that yew for three years, but I...'

At the bottom of the hole left by the yew, Saha sensed a mole; she could see it in her head, if not smell it. For a minute she forgot herself, she went mad, and began digging frantically like a fox terrier, rolling over like a lizard, leaping up with her four paws like a toad; she held a clod of earth between her legs like a field rat protecting a stolen egg, and then freed herself from the hole by a series of wondrous manoeuvres and sat down on the lawn, coolly and primly recovering her breath.

Alain watched gravely, without moving. He knew he must be serious when Saha's demons drew her beyond herself. His admiration and understanding of the cat were innate in him, and these essentials gave him the ability to interpret Saha easily. He read her like a book, ever since that day when, after leaving a cat show, he had placed a kitten of five months on the mown lawn of Neuilly, purchased because of her perfect face, because of her grown-up self-possession and long-suffering dignity behind the bars of a cage.

'Why didn't you buy an angora instead?' Camille asked.

'She called me *vous* in those days,'* Alain remembered. 'But It wasn't just a little cat that I got. It was a noble feline, utterly indifferent to everything, self-assured, those qualities she has in common with the very best of humans...' He reddened and then apologetically corrected himself. 'Saha, the very best humans understand you best of all.'

He had not yet gone as far as to say 'resemble you' instead of 'understand you' for he belonged to a tribe which forbids itself to recognize or even conceive of a kinship with animals. But at the age when most young men might have coveted a motor car, a trip abroad, a rare book or a pair of skis, Alain was still the 'young-man-who-bought-a-kitten'. His narrow entourage exclaimed about it, the employees of the Maison Amparat et Fils, Rue des Petits-Champs, couldn't get over it and Monsieur Veuillet asked Alain after 'that little monster'.

'Before I chose you, Saha, I perhaps would never have realized one can choose anything. As to the rest, my wedding makes everyone happy including Camille and at times I'm happy about it too, but...'

He rose from the green bench, assumed the self-satisfied smile of the son of the Amparats who was about to condescend to wed the daughter of the Malmert launderers, 'a young lady, not quite our sort', as Madame Amparat said. But Alain knew very well that the Malmerts, who were in the washing-machine business, speaking among themselves about the Amparats, who were in the silk trade, were sure to remark, with a lifting of the chin: 'The Amparats aren't in the silk trade any more, the mother and son just keep a stake in the house, and the son isn't running it.'

Now over her wild excesses, the cat, her eyes soft and golden, seemed to be waiting to regain her mental composure, and pricked up her silver-edged ear at his telepathic murmurings.

'And you're not just a pure and shining example of a cat either,' Alain went on. 'Your first lover, that white moggy without a tail, if you remember, you naughty girl, my fine lady, my little tramp in the rain...'

'Your cat's such a bad mother!' cried Camille, indignant. 'She's forgotten all about the kittens they took away from her!'

'But that's just what a young woman would say,' Alain went on, mistrustfully. 'Young women always *are* good mothers, before...'

The sound of a bell, full and solemn, was heard on the quiet air and Alain got up with a guilty jump at the noise of gravel crushed beneath the wheels of a car.

'Camille! Oh, my goodness, it's half past eleven.'

He pulled his pyjama top across his chest and tightened the belt with such a trembling hand that he chided himself. 'Come on, what's the matter with me? I'll be seeing plenty more of them in a week... Saha, are you coming to meet her?'

But Saha had disappeared, and Camille was already walking imperiously over the lawn. 'Ah, she's a real good-looker...' He felt a pleasant stirring in his blood, and his throat tightened, the colour came into his cheeks, and he was completely absorbed by the sight of Camille in white, the black wisps of her well-trimmed hair at her temples, a thin red scarf tied round her neck, and matching red on her lips. Her make-up was elegant and discreet, her youthfulness only became evident after a moment or two, revealing a white cheek under the ochre skin, the smooth unlined eyelids with a touch of beige powder around her large, almost black eyes. The brand-new diamond on her left hand fractured the light into a thousand coloured sparks.

'Oh!' she cried. 'You're not ready! In such lovely weather!'

But she stopped when she saw the rough disorder of his blond hair, the bare chest beneath his pyjamas, the embarrassment which made Alain blush, and the whole expression on her young face so clearly showed her warm womanly indulgence, that Alain no longer dared give her the quarter-to-twelve kiss, the one in the garden or the Bois.

'Kiss me,' she begged under her breath, as though asking him for help.

Awkward, uneasy, and defenceless beneath his thin pyjamas, he pointed silently to the pink flowering bushes, through which came the sound of secateurs and rake, and Camille did not dare throw her arms around him. She looked down, plucked a leaf, rearranged the glossy strands of hair on her cheek, but by the movement of her nostrils, Alain could see she was sniffing the air like an animal, scenting his fair skin, only just concealed, which privately he thought her not sufficiently in awe of.

3

WHEN he woke, he didn't sit up in bed straight away. Haunted in his sleep by the unfamiliar bedroom, he half opened his eyes, feeling that subterfuge and constraint had not altogether deserted him while he slept, for his extended left arm, assigned to the confines of the white steppes of the sheets, lay ready to register where he was and also to fend off that realization...But the whole of the vast bed on his left-hand side was empty and cool. Had it not been for the barely rounded corner of the three-walled bedroom, the unusual green darkness, and the yellow line of light like an amber rod separating the vertical shadow of the two dark curtains facing the bed, Alain would have dozed off again, rocked to sleep moreover by someone quietly humming a little negro spiritual.

He turned his head cautiously, opened his eyes and saw, now white and now light blue, according to whether she was bathing in the narrow stream of sunshine or whether she had come back into the shadows, a naked young woman with a comb in her hand and a cigarette in her mouth, humming a tune. 'What a nerve!' he thought. 'Stark naked? Where does she think she is?'

He recognized her beautiful legs—they had been familiar to him for a long time—but her belly, shortened by her slightly low navel, astonished him. Her muscular buttocks were made acceptable by an impersonal youthfulness, and her breasts were light above her visible ribs. 'So, she's got thinner?' Her substantial back, broad as her chest, was a shock to Alain. 'She has a common back...' And indeed at that moment Camille leaned on one of the windows, arched her back, and lifted her shoulders. 'She's got the back of a charwoman.' But she suddenly stood up, took two dancing strides and, with a charming gesture, embraced the thin air. 'No, it's not true, she's beautiful. But what a...what a nerve! Does she imagine I'm dead? Or does she think it's perfectly natural to cavort around stark naked? Oh, that will have to change...'

As she turned towards the bed, he shut his eyes again. When he opened them, Camille was seated at the dressing table which they called the 'invisible dressing table', a transparent shelf of beautiful thick cut glass resting on a black metal stand. She powdered her face, felt her cheek and chin with the tips of her fingers, and gave a sudden smile as she looked away with a seriousness and lassitude that disarmed Alain. 'Is she happy then? What can she be happy about? I don't deserve it...But why is she naked?'

'Camille!' he cried.

He thought she would escape to the bathroom, shield her sex with her hands, cover her breasts with a veil of some crumpled lingerie; but instead she ran to the bed, leaned over the young man, and from out of the hiding-places of her armpits and the covert of dark blue algae that bloomed on her insignificant little belly, brought him her strong smell of brunette.

'My darling! Did you sleep well?'

You're all naked!' he scolded.

She opened her wide eyes even larger, mocking him.

'So what! What about you?'

He was bare to the waist and had no answer to that. So far from being embarrassed, she flaunted herself so proudly in front of him, that rather abruptly he threw her the pyjamas lying crumpled on the bed.

'Quick! Put these on! I'm famished!'

'Mother Buque is at her post! Everything's in order and working!'

She vanished and Alain tried to get up, put on his clothes, smooth his rumpled hair, but Camille came back with a large dressing gown tied round her, new and too long for her. She was in high spirits and carried a loaded tray.

'What a mess, my dears! There's a bowl, a pyrex cup, sugar in the lid of a tin...But we'll sort it all out; my ham's dry...These anaemic-looking peaches are the leftovers from lunch...Mother Buque is rather out of her depth in her electrified kitchen. I'll teach her how to manage the fuses. And I poured some water in the ice compartments of the fridge...Oh what would she do without me! Monsieur has very hot coffee and boiling milk, and hard butter...No, that's my tea, don't touch! What are you looking for?'

'No, nothing.'

Because of the smell of coffee, he was looking for Saha.

'What time is it?'

'Ha, so you are being nice to me at last!' Camille cried. 'It's very early, husband of mine. The kitchen clock said a quarter past eight.'

They breakfasted, with much merriment and little conversation. By the increasingly warm smell from the green oilcloth curtains, Alain could guess at the strength of the sun, and could not stop thinking about the sunshine outside, the strange horizon, the nine vertiginous storeys, the odd architecture of the Quart-de-Brie which was their temporary home.

He listened to Camille as well as he could, touched that she pretended to have forgotten what had taken place between them that night, as though she were a long-term resident in this random lodging, and a married woman of at least one week's standing. Now that she had something on, he was wondering how he could show her how grateful he was. 'She doesn't hold it against me, either for what I have or what I haven't done, the poor girl. But the worst is over. Is it often like this the first night, this "nothing very special", this bruising? This semi-success, semi-disaster...'

In an affectionate way he put his arm around her shoulders and kissed her.

'Oh, you're such a kind boy!'

She said it so loud and with such feeling that he perceived that her eyes were full of tears. But bravely she fought her emotion and jumped out of bed on the pretext of taking away the tray. She hurried to the window, tripped over her dressing gown that was too long, uttered a coarse oath and clung on to a curtain cord like a ship's rope. The oilcloth curtains opened. Paris, with its *banlieue*,* bluish and limitless like the desert, with patches of verdure that were still bright, and flashes of beetle-blue panes, came leaping into the triangular bedroom, which had only one concrete wall, the others being half glazed.

'Beautiful,' said Alain, uncertainly.

But he was not quite telling the truth, and his head was seeking the support of a young shoulder from which the towelling bathrobe had slipped. 'This isn't a lodging for humans...All that horizon here, in this bed! And what about the days when it's stormy? Abandoned at the top of a lighthouse among the albatrosses...'

Camille's arm, for she had joined him again on the bed, was under his neck, and she looked calmly at the vertiginous expanses of Paris and the blond, dishevelled hair. This new pride of hers, which seemed to have faith in the night after and the days that were to follow, was no doubt happy with today's liberties: rumpling the communal bed, supporting a naked young male body with her shoulder and hips, getting used to his colour, his curves, his irritations, staring boldly and lengthily at the small dry nipples, the hips that she envied, the strange design of the capricious male organ...

They bit into the same insipid peach and laughed as they showed each other their lovely glistening teeth, their pale gums, like those of tired children.

'What a day yesterday!' Camille sighed. 'When you think there are people who get married often!'

Vanity returned and she added:

'But it was really good, wasn't it? Nothing went wrong, did it?'

'No,' replied Alain, faintly.

'Oh you! Just like your mother! I mean, providing people didn't ruin the lawn or throw cigarette butts all over the gravel path, you would both think it had gone well. Isn't that right? Which isn't to say that our wedding wouldn't have been nicer at Neuilly. Except that it would have disturbed the sainted feline...Tell me, naughty boy, what are you looking at around you?'

'Nothing,' he answered honestly. 'There's nothing to see. I've seen the dressing table, the chair, we've seen the bed...'

'Could you not live here? I like it here a lot. Just think! Three rooms, three balconies. Suppose one stayed?'

'One says: "Suppose we stayed?"'

'So why in that case do you say: "One says?" Yes, suppose we stayed, as *we* were saying.'

'But Patrick is coming back from his cruise in three months' time.'

'So what? He comes back. We tell him we want to stay. And we throw him out.'

'Oh, could you do that?'

Radiantly at ease in her female unscrupulousness, she shook her black mop of hair in assent. Alain attempted a frown, but at his look of disapproval, Camille changed and became anxious, just as he himself felt anxious, and so he quickly kissed her on the mouth.

Silenced, hurriedly, she returned his kiss and searched for the dip in the bed with a movement of her hips. At the same time, her free hand clutching a peach stone felt blindly in the air for an empty cup or ashtray.

Leaning over his companion, he waited, stroking her, until she opened her eyes again. Her lids were squeezed tight over two little glistening tears trying not to creep out, and he respected her discretion and pride. They had done their best, she and he, in silence, helped by the morning warmth, by their two scented, compliant bodies.

Alain remembered Camille's breathing getting more and more rapid and it crossed his mind that she had been warm and submissive with him, in a rather untimely eagerness that he liked very much. She was not like any other woman he had known; his one concern, possessing her for the second time, was to be gentle with her, as she deserved. She lay next to him, her arms and legs softly bent, her hands half closed, and for the first time she resembled a cat. 'Where *is* Saha?'

Mechanically he gave Camille the hint of a kiss, for Saha, his nails lightly scraping along her belly. She cried out in shock, her arms stiffened and one hit Alain, who almost hit her back. Sitting up, surveying him in a hostile fashion from beneath her tousled hair, Camille gave him a threatening look:

'Might you be a bit perverted, by any chance?'

He wasn't expecting anything like that and burst out laughing.

'It's not funny!' cried Camille. 'I've always been told men who tickle women are depraved, or even sadistic!'

He got out of bed to be able to laugh more easily, forgetting he didn't have any clothes on. Camille was so suddenly silent that he turned around and surprised her look of open amazement, attentive to everything about this young man whom a night of marriage had just offered her.

'I'll use the bathroom for ten minutes, if that's all right.'

He opened the mirrored door set into one of the ends of the longest wall they called the hypotenuse.

'And then I'll go and see my mother for a minute or two.'

'All right. Wouldn't you like me to come with you?'

He seemed taken aback and she blushed, the first time that day.

'I'll see if the building works...'

'Oh, the building works! Are you really interested in the building works? Confess,' and she crossed her arms like a tragic actress, 'confess you are going to see my rival!'

'Saha's not your rival,' Alain said flatly.

'How could she possibly be your rival,' he went on in his head. 'Only among the impure could you have rivals.'

'You don't have to protest so violently, darling. Go quickly! And don't forget we are lunching at Leopold's, just the two of us...Just us two! Will you be back home soon? Don't forget we are going to try out the motor? Are you listening to me?'

What he mainly took in was that her saying 'home' had assumed a new significance, ludicrous and perhaps unacceptable, and he looked askance at Camille. She was flaunting her newly married tiredness, the slight swelling of her lower eyelids in the corner of her wide eyes.

'Will you always have, no matter what time of the day, such wide eyes as soon as you wake up? Can't you half close your eyes? Seeing eyes so wide open makes my head ache.'

He supposed it rather a dishonest pleasure, an easy, evasive tactic, to ask her questions without uttering them aloud. 'Well, it's not so rude as being honest with her, when all's said and done.' He hurried towards the square bathtub, the hot water, to be on his own where he could better meditate. But as the mirror let into the door of the hypotenuse reflected him from head to toe, Alain opened it slowly and in a leisurely fashion and was in no rush to close it again.

When he left the flat an hour later he went out of the wrong door, on to one of the balconies in the Quart-de-Brie, and received the full force of the east wind which was turning Paris blue, carrying away the smoke and stripping clean the Sacré-Cœur. On the concrete parapet were five or six pots, placed there by well-intentioned hands, containing white roses, hydrangeas, lilies yellowed by their pollen...'Last night's dessert is never as nice...' Nevertheless, before going down, he moved the battered flowers out of the wind.

4

HE entered the garden like an adolescent who has spent the night out. The potent smell of the compost heaps being watered, the secret vapours of the disgusting things that nourish the luxurious and expensive flowers, the pearls of water chased away by the breeze, he breathed them all in and discovered at the same moment that he needed comforting.

'Saha! Saha!'

She took her time coming and he did not immediately recognize her lost, unbelieving expression that looked shrouded in a bad dream.

'Saha, my darling!'

He held her against his chest, stroking her soft flanks, which he thought a little thin, and brushing away some silky cobwebs as well as bits of pine and elm from her unwashed fur. She recovered rapidly and resumed the customary dignified expression in her pure golden eyes. Beneath his thumbs Alain could feel the small hard irregular heartbeat and the hesitant beginnings of a purr. He put her down on a wrought-iron table and stroked her. But the moment she thrust her head into Alain's hand in that wild way of hers, as though it would be for ever, she caught its scent and backed away.

He was looking to see if he could catch sight of the white pigeon, the gloved hand behind the bushes with the pink clusters of flowers, behind the blazing rhododendrons. He was delighted that yesterday's 'ceremony', keeping out of this beautiful garden, had caused havoc only in Camille's place.

'Those people here...And those four pink bridesmaids...And the flowers they would have picked, and the deutzias sacrificed for the corsages of those fat ladies...And Saha...'

He shouted in the direction of the house:

'Has Saha had something to eat and drink? She looks a bit odd. I'm here, Maman.'

At the entrance to the hall a thick white silhouette appeared and answered from a distance.

'No, actually, she hasn't. She hasn't had her food nor her milk this morning. I think she's been waiting for you. How are you, my son?'

He stood at the bottom of the steps respectfully. He noticed his mother didn't hold out her cheek to be kissed as she usually did, and that she kept her hands clasped against her belt. He understood and shared with embarrassment and gratitude this motherly reticence.

'Saha didn't kiss me either.'

'Well, the cat has seen you go off many times. She knows she has to accept your absences.'

'But I didn't move so very far,' he thought.

Near him on the iron table, Saha drank her milk greedily like an animal that has walked a long way and slept little.

'You don't want a cup of hot milk too, Alain? Some bread and butter?'

'I've had breakfast, Maman...We've had breakfast.'

'Not much of a breakfast, I imagine, in a *caravansérail* like that.'

Alain smiled, because his mother always said *caravansérail* when she meant *capharnaüm*.*

With the eye of an exile he contemplated the cup with the gold arabesque next to Saha's saucer, then his mother's coarse, kindly face beneath her fuzz of prematurely white hair.

'I haven't asked you if my new daughter is happy...'

She was suddenly afraid he might have misunderstood and added hurriedly:

'I mean, if she is well?'

'Very well, Maman...We're going to have lunch in the forest of Rambouillet, I'm going to try...'

He corrected himself:

'*We're* going to try the car out, I mean...'

Saha and Alain were alone in the garden, both numb with fatigue, with silence, summoned by sleep.

The cat fell asleep abruptly on her side, chin in the air, her teeth bared like a dead tiger; feathery florets from the smoke tree, petals from the clematis, dropped on her without disturbing the deep dreams in which she was no doubt relishing the safety, the inalienable presence of her friend. Her exhausted attitude, the drawn, pale corners of her bluey-grey lips were evidence she had spent a miserable night watching out for him.

At the top of the dried-out trunk draped with climbers, a swarm of bees on the flowering ivy kept up a low thrumming sound, as they had for so many summers. 'If I could sleep here on the grass between the yellow rose and the cat…Camille wouldn't come till dinner, it would be lovely…And the cat, oh, my goodness, the cat…' Over by the 'building works', a plane was shaving a plank of wood, an iron hammer was banging on a metal girder, and already Alain in his imagination was dreaming of a mysterious village populated with blacksmiths… When eleven o'clock struck from the bell-tower of a school, he stood up and escaped without daring to wake the cat.

5

JUNE and the longer days arrived with their luminous night skies, brightened at each end by a late gleam of sunset and a streak of light rising over the east of Paris. But June is only cruel if you are a town dweller without a car, imprisoned by hot stone walls, everyone in close proximity to one another. Around the Quart-de-Brie, the constant breeze agitated the yellow blinds, crossed the triangle and the living room, collided with the prow of the building and dried out the little hedges of privet in their tubs on the terraces. Helped by their daily outings, Alain and Camille lived quietly, calm and drowsy with the warmth and with their pleasure.

'Why did I call her an incorrigible young woman?' Alain wondered. Camille wasn't swearing so much when she was behind the wheel, her sharp tongue was softening, as was her appetite for clubs where young gypsy women with flared nostrils sang their songs.

She ate and slept a lot, opened her soft eyes very wide, disregarded a score of plans for the summer, and took an interest in the 'building works' which she visited each day. Sometimes she lingered a long time in the Jardin de Neuilly, where Alain, on leaving the dark offices of Maison Amparat et Fils in the Rue des Petits-Champs would find her at a loose end, ready to make the afternoon last longer and go for a drive along the hot roads.

Then he grew more disgruntled. He heard her giving orders to the singing painters and distant electricians. She would question him in a general and peremptory manner, as though it was her duty, and as soon as he was there, she abandoned her new placidity.

'How's business? Is the crisis still threatening? Have you flogged any spotty cloth to the princes of fashion?'

She didn't even have any respect for old Émile whom she pestered until he came out with platitudes of an oracular imbecility.

'What do you think of our glory hole, Émile? You've never seen the house look so beautiful?'

Through his whiskers the old valet mumbled responses that, like himself, had no meaning or colour.

'You wouldn't know the place...If you'd told me before that the house would be divided up into little boxes...It's all different now. We'll be all together, all of us, very jolly.'

Or, drop by drop, he would pour blessings upon Alain, which concealed a certain hostility.

'Monsieur Alain's young lady looks well. And she has a fine voice. You can hear every word from the neighbour's house. A voice not to be disobeyed, oh no! But the young lady certainly says what she means. She was telling the gardener that the bed of privet and forget-me-nots looked silly…I'm still laughing about it.'

And he raised his pale eyes to heaven. They were oyster grey and had never laughed. Alain wasn't laughing either. Saha was causing him concern. She was getting thinner and appeared to be losing hope, probably the hope of seeing Alain again every day, just the two of them. She no longer ran off when Camille arrived. But she didn't go to the gate with Alain, and she watched him when he sat next to her, with a deep and bitter look of wisdom. 'The same look from behind the bars of the cage when she was a kitten, exactly the same look.' He called softly to her: 'Saha, Saha…', breathing out the 'h' very loud. But she didn't leap about, or put her ears down, and for many days she hadn't made her loud 'Me-rrang' noise nor the 'mouek mouek mouek' of good humour and desire.

One day when they—Camille and himself—had been summoned to Neuilly to be told that the new square, heavy, enormous bathtub would cause the supporting floor to collapse, he heard his wife sigh:

'Oh, it'll never be finished!'

'But', he said, in surprise, 'I thought you were happier in the Quart-de-Brie anyway, with the cormorants and petrels…'

'Yes…But all the same…And in any case, this is your house, here, your real house…Our house…'

She leaned on his arm, a bit frail and unusually for her, uncertain. The light blue of her eyes, almost as blue as her bright summer dress, the perfect, unnecessary make-up on her cheek, mouth and eyebrows, did not touch him.

Yet it seemed to him that for the first time she was implicitly asking his opinion. 'Camille here with me! Already! Camille in pyjamas under the rose arbour…' One of the oldest rosebushes bore at eye level its burden of roses which lost their colour as soon as they bloomed, and their oriental scent pervaded the whole place, even as far as the steps. 'Camille in her bathrobe under the elm-tree walk…' Would it not be better, when all was said and done, to keep her there in the little belvedere still, in the Quart-de Brie? 'Not here, not here—not yet…'

The June evening, saturated with light, was taking its time to decide in favour of night. Empty glasses on a wicker table kept the fat rust-coloured bumblebees busy, but beneath the trees, except under the pines, there spread an indefinable aura of dampness, the promise of freshness to come. Neither the rose geraniums, exuding scents of the South, nor the blazing poppies were suffering from the unforgiving summer that was on the way. 'Not here, not here...', Alain beat out the words in time with his steps. Looking for Saha, but not wanting to call her, he found her lying on the little low wall which was supporting a mound covered with blue lobelia. She was asleep, or appeared to be, curled up in a ball. 'In a ball? At this time of day and in weather like this? Curled up like that, asleep, is a winter position...'.

'Saha darling!'

She did not wince when he reached down and lifted her up, and she opened her vacant eyes, very beautiful, almost indifferent.

'Goodness, you weigh nothing! Are you poorly, my little tiger?'

He took her in his arms and hurried over to his mother and Camille.

'Maman, Saha is ill! Her fur is dull, she weighs nothing, and you didn't tell me!'

'Because she's hardly eating anything,' said Madame Amparat. 'She doesn't want to eat.'

'She's not eating, is anything else wrong?'

He was nursing the cat against his chest and Saha was abandoning herself to him, her breathing short and her nostrils dry. Madame Amparat's eyes, under her mop of curly white hair, looked meaning-fully in Camille's direction.

'Nothing else,' she said.

'She's pining for you,' said Camille. 'She's your cat, isn't she?'

He thought she was having a joke at his expense and raised his head defiantly. But Camille's expression hadn't changed, and she was look-ing curiously at the cat, who, at her touch, shut her eyes again.

'Feel her ears,' said Alain abruptly. 'They're burning.'

He hesitated only for a second.

'Ok, I'll take her with me. Maman, could you get her basket for me? And a bag of sand for the tray. Apart from that we have everything we need. You realize I absolutely don't want... This cat thinks that...'

He broke off and turned rather belatedly to his wife.

'Camille, you don't mind if I take Saha back while we are waiting to move here?'

'What a question! But where are you going to put her at night?' she added, so naïvely, that Alain blushed because his mother was present, and he answered sharply:

'She can choose where.'

They set off in a little procession, Alain carrying the silent Saha in her travelling basket. Old Émile was bending under the weight of the full bag of sand, and Camille brought up the rear, in charge of the ancient, frayed cashmere blanket Alain called the Cashasaha.

6

'No, I never thought a cat would get used to it so quickly...'

'A cat is just a cat. But Saha is Saha.'

Proudly Alain was attending to Saha. He himself had never held her captive in such confined surroundings, twenty-five square metres, on show at all times and reduced, for feline meditation or desire for shade and solitude, to hiding under the gigantic armchairs that shifted from place to place in the living room, or in what passed for an entrance hall, or in one of the coat cupboards camouflaged with mirrors.

But Saha was determined to overcome all obstacles. She accommodated herself to mealtimes, which were variable, to bedtime and getting-up time, elected to spend the night in the bathroom on her sponge-topped stool, and explored the Quart-de-Brie without appearing disgusted or antisocial. She condescended to listen to Madame Buque's futile invitations to 'puss' to eat some raw liver. When Alain and Camille had gone out, she took up a position on the vertiginous parapet and surveyed the abyss of space, unconcernedly gazing at the backs of the swallows and sparrows flying beneath her. Her impassivity on the edge of the nine storeys, the habit she adopted of washing herself lengthily on the parapet, drove Camille wild.

'Stop her!' she shouted to Alain. 'It's making my stomach turn over and I'm getting cramps in my legs!'

Alain, the expert, smiled admiringly at his cat, who had now recovered her zest for life and food.

It was not that she suddenly grew healthier or so very lively. Her iridescent fur, mauve as pigeon's feathers, had not returned. But she had started to enjoy life more, waiting for the dull thud of the lift hauling Alain upstairs, and accepting odd treats offered by Camille, such as a tiny saucer of milk, a little chicken bone which she held in her hand as you do when you are trying to make a dog jump up.

'Not like that, like this!' Alain scolded.

And he would place the chicken on a bathmat or directly on the beige pile carpet.

'Poor Patrick's carpet!' tut-tutted Camille.

'A cat never eats a bone or piece of meat on a polished surface. When a cat takes a bone out of a plate and puts it on the carpet before eating it, we tell her she's messy. But a cat needs to keep her prey under her paw while she crushes or tears it apart, and she can only do that on the bare earth or on a carpet. But people don't know that.'

Camille, astonished, interrupted him.

'And how do you know?'

Never having wondered how he had acquired the knowledge, he avoided a straight answer by joking:

'Hush! It's because I'm so clever. Don't tell anyone! Monsieur Veuillet doesn't know.'

He instructed her in the ways and habits of felines as though it were a foreign language rich in a wealth of subtleties. Despite himself he was very vehement when he held forth. Camille observed him narrowly and asked him a score of questions, which he promptly answered.

'Why does the cat play with string if she's afraid of the big cord that works the curtains?'

'Because to her the cord is a snake. It's the same thickness as a snake. She's afraid of snakes.'

'Has she ever seen a snake?'

Alain looked at his wife out of his grey-green eyes with the black lashes that she thought so beautiful, 'so dastardly', as she said.

'No, certainly not. Where would she have seen one?'

'So then?'

'So she invents it. She creates it. You'd be afraid of a snake too, even if you hadn't seen one.'

'Yes, but I've been told about them, I've seen pictures of them. I know they exist.'

'Saha does too.'

'How?'

He flashed her an imperious smile.

'How? She just knows, like the person of quality she is.'

'So, am I not a person of quality?'

He grew more gentle, but only because he was sorry for her.

'No, no, don't be upset: I'm not either. You don't really believe all I tell you?'

Sitting at her husband's feet, Camille looked at him with her enormous eyes, the eyes of the little girl of long ago who did not want to say hello.

'I have to believe you,' she said gravely.

They sat down to dinner almost every evening at home, because of the heat, Alain said, 'and because of Saha', insinuated Camille. One evening after dinner, Saha was sitting on her friend's knee.

'What about me?' Camille said.

'I've got two knees,' Alain rejoined.

In any case the cat didn't take advantage of this privilege for very long. Answering some mysterious call, she went back to her polished ebony table, sat down on her own bluish reflection immersed in a shadowy pool and nothing in her would have seemed out of character except for the fixed attention she was giving to invisible presences in front of her in space.

'What's she staring at?' Camille asked.

At the same time each evening she looked pretty in her white pyjamas, her hair half undone and loose on her forehead, her cheeks very brown beneath the layers of powder she had plastered over them since getting up. Alain sometimes kept his summer outfit on, without a waistcoat, but Camille's hands fussed over him, took his jacket off, his tie, undid his shirt, rolled up the sleeves, revealed and explored his naked flesh, and he told her she was a bold hussy, but let her do it. She laughed somewhat sorrowfully, trying to control her desire. And it was he who looked down to hide an apprehension which was not exclusively voluptuous: 'What ravages of desire on her face…Her lips are all tight—such a young woman…Who taught her to anticipate me like that?'

The round table, with a little trolley on rubber wheels next to it, saw them all together on the edge of the living room near the open bay window. Three tall ancient poplars, the flotsam of a beautiful garden now destroyed, were waving their heads at terrace height, and the vast Paris sun, dark red, smothered in mist, was setting behind their slender tops from which the sap was retreating.

Madame Buque's supper, served badly but cooked well, brightened the hour. Alain was restored, and forgot about his day and the Amparat office, and being supervised by Monsieur Veuillet. His two captives of the belvedere celebrated his arrival. 'Were you waiting for me?' he whispered in Saha's ear.

'I heard you coming!' Camille cried. 'You can hear everything from up here!'

'Have you been bored?' he asked her one evening, fearing she might complain. But she shook her black mop of hair in denial.

'Not the least bit! I went to see Maman. She introduced me to the treasure.'

'What treasure?'

'The girl who will be my maid when we move. Provided that old Émile doesn't get her pregnant! She's very pretty.'

She laughed, rolling up her wide white crêpe sleeves, before she cut into the red melon. Saha was hovering. But Alain didn't laugh, being absolutely horrified at the thought of a new servant in his house.

'Really? Well, did you know', he confessed, 'that my mother has never changed her staff since I was a little boy...'

'So much is obvious,' cut in Camille. 'It's a real museum!'

She was nibbling at the skin of a crescent of melon and was laughing, facing against the sunset. Alain admired, without any especial sympathy, how Camille's face lit up with a kind of man-eating vivacity, her eyes sparkling, her mouth narrow, and something Italian about her expression. He made another effort to see things from her point of view.

'It appears you don't see your girlfriends nowadays? Perhaps you could...'

'Which girlfriends would that be?' she demanded, piqued. 'Are you trying to tell me I'm getting in your way? I should give myself a bit of space? That right?'

He raised his eyebrows, tut-tutted disapproval, and she gave way at once, with plebeian respect for his masculine scorn.

'Well, it's true. I hardly had any friends when I was a little girl. And now...Can you see me friends with a girl? Either I'd have to treat her like a child, or answer all her sordid questions: "How do you do that or how does he do that to you?" Girls,' she explained, and there was a bitter tone in her voice, 'girls aren't very honest with one another. No solidarity. Not like with you men.'

'Excuse me! I am not one of *you men*!'

'Oh, I know,' she said sadly. 'And sometimes I wonder if I shouldn't prefer...'

She wasn't often affected by melancholy, she was only cast down when she was harbouring something in secret or had doubts that she didn't express.

'Well, you've got scarcely any friends either,' she went on, 'apart from Patrick who is not here. And you don't even really care much about Patrick.'

At a gesture from Alain she broke off.

'Don't let's talk about those things,' she said, 'or we'll fall out.'

Long cries of children reached them from down below, like the sharp twittering of swallows. Saha's beautiful yellow eyes were gradually widening as her pupils changed to their night-time mode, and she was staring into space at shifting, invisible, floating spots.

'Tell me what that cat's looking at, will you? There's nothing there, is there, what's she looking at?'

'Nothing that we can see.'

Alain was thinking about, missing the little thrill, the seductive fear infused into him by his cat-friend, before, when she slept at nights on his chest.

'At least you're not afraid of her?' he suggested patronizingly.

Camille burst out laughing as though that insult was just what she was waiting for.

'Afraid? I'm not afraid of anything very much, as you know.'

'You're a little fool to say things like that,' said Alain, annoyed.

'Let's just say', Camille said with a shrug, 'that the storm clouds are gathering…'

She pointed to the purple bank of cloud which was rising as night fell.

'And you are just like Saha,' she added. 'You don't care for storms.'

'No one likes storms.'

'I don't mind them,' said Camille, in a fervent tone. 'Well, I'm not scared of them anyway.'

'Everybody's afraid of storms,' said Alain coldly.

'Well, I'm not everybody, so that's that.'

'Oh yes, you are to me,' he answered, with a sudden and insincere charm, which did not fool her for a moment.

'Oh,' she muttered, 'I could hit you…'

He let his blond hair fall over the table, and his white teeth gleamed. 'Hit me!'

But she deprived herself of the pleasure of rumpling those gold locks, of surrendering her naked arm to that gleaming mouth.

'Your nose is crooked,' she said, to be cruel.

'It must be the thunderstorm,' he laughed.

Camille did not think much of this response, but the first low rumblings of thunder distracted her. She threw her serviette aside and ran on to the terrace.

'Come out here! We'll see the lightning start to flash—so beautiful!'

'No,' said Alain, not moving, 'you come.'

'Where?'

He pointed to the bedroom with his chin. On Camille's face formed the mulish expression, the obtuse desire that he knew so well, and yet she hesitated:

'Shall we look at the lightning first?'

He shook his head.

'Why not, wicked boy?'

'Because I'm afraid of thunderstorms. You choose. Thunderstorm or me.'

'Oh, well in *that* case!'

She ran to their bedroom with an enthusiasm that filled Alain with pride. But as he joined her he saw she had deliberately lit a small glass lamp near the huge bed, and just as deliberately he put it out.

Through the open bay windows, the warm rain, scented with ozone, came whipping in, whilst they sought relief in each other's arms. Camille made him understand that she would have liked, while the storm was gathering, that with her he would forget his fear of the thunderstorm. But he was nervously counting the huge sheets of lightning and the tall dazzling trees silhouetted against the clouds, and he drew away from Camille. She resigned herself, propped herself on one elbow and ran her hand through the crisping hair of her husband. At the tremors of the lightning their faces, like two pale blue plaster-casts, loomed up out of the darkness and then were lost again.

'Let's wait till the storm is over,' she decided.

'There you are,' Alain said to himself. 'That's what she says after an encounter that would indeed have been worth it. She might have kept quiet at least. As Émile says, "the young lady says what she means..."'

A rapid series of flashes, the time it takes to have a dream, was reflected in a fiery strip on the thick slice of crystal on the invisible dressing table; Camille squeezed against Alain with her bare leg.

'Are you trying to comfort me? I know you're not afraid of thunder.'

He raised his voice so that he could be heard above the resounding thunderclaps and the cascades of rain on the flat roof. He felt tired and annoyed, ready to make unfair remarks, alarmed to realize that he would never be alone any more. Violently he cast his mind back to his old room, papered in conventional white flower-patterned wallpaper, the bedroom that no hand had ever attempted to decorate or spoil. His desire was so keen that the flat, clear flowers he could visualize were succeeded by the hum of the old stove that did not work properly, its murmur like the breathing of a dry cellar, issuing from a copper-lipped mouth built into the parquet floor. A hum that joined the hum of the whole house, the whispering of old servants worn out by constant work, buried up to their waist in their basement, and no longer even tempted to go out in the garden. 'They said "She" when they referred to my mother, but from the time I was in long trousers I was always "Monsieur Alain".'

A sudden clap of thunder recalled him from the brief sleep he had slipped into gratefully. His young wife leaning over him, propped up on her elbow, had not moved.

'I love you when you're asleep,' she said. 'The storm's subsiding.'

He took this as a request and sat up.

'I'm doing the same,' he said. 'How hot and sticky it is! I'm going to go and sleep on the bench in the waiting room.'

That's what they called the narrow couch, the only piece of furniture in a small hybrid sort of room, a passage with glazed windows that Patrick intended for heliotherapy sessions.

'Oh no, oh no, stay here!' Camille begged.

But he was already sliding out of bed. The bright light from the clouds revealed the hard, offended expression of Camille.

'Pooh! Stupid little boy!'

And with this unexpected exclamation, she tweaked his nose. Bringing the back of his arm up instinctively, he knocked her disrespectful hand away and did not regret it. A sudden cessation of the wind and rain left them alone in their silence and as if deaf. Camille was massaging her numb hand.

'You are a brute,' Camille said finally.

'Possibly,' Alain said. 'I don't like people touching my face. Isn't the rest of me enough? Don't ever touch my face.'

'Yes, you are,' Camille slowly repeated. 'You are a brute.'

'Don't say that too often. Apart from that, I don't bear you any grudge. But be careful.'

He pulled his bare leg back under the bedclothes.

'Can you see that big grey square on the carpet? That's dawn. Do you want to go to sleep?'

'Yes, I want to sleep…', said the same uncertain voice.

'Well then, come here!'

He stretched out his left arm for her to rest her head and with a guarded politeness she meekly complied. Pleased with himself, Alain gave her an amicable shove and pulled her towards him, but gave her some space, just in case, by drawing his knees up slightly, and fell straight away into a sleep. Wide awake, Camille lay breathing quietly, her eyes fixed on the grey pool on the carpet which was getting lighter. She listened to the sparrows celebrating the end of the storm in the three poplars whose swishing sounded like the downpour itself. When Alain changed position and took his arm away, he caressed her head three times, unconsciously, in a way that seemed more used to stroking fur that was even softer than her own soft black hair.

7

IT was towards the end of June that between them their incompatibility established itself like a new season, with its surprises and occasional delights. Alain breathed it in like a sharp spring taking up residence in the middle of summer. He carried with him his aversion to establishing a position for the foreign young woman in the house where he was born, he concealed this effortlessly, but kept it brewing mysteriously inside by soliloquies and by the covert contemplation of the new conjugal apartment. One day when the heat was stifling, on their high bridge deserted by the wind, Camille cried out in exasperation:

'Oh, let's ditch everything! Let's take the car and go for a bathe somewhere! What do you say, Alain?'

'I'm with you,' he replied with a wily promptness. 'Where shall we go?'

He had some respite while Camille recited the names of beaches and hotels. Looking at Saha lying flat on the floor, he took time to reflect and concluded:

'I don't want to go away with her. I...I don't dare. I don't mind going out like we are doing at the moment, coming back in the evening or late at night. But that's all. I don't want to spend evenings in a hotel, or a casino, evenings...' He gave a little shudder: 'I need time, I know it's taking me a long time to get used to it, and that I'm not easy to live with...But I don't want to go travelling with her.' He felt a momentary pang when he realized he was saying 'her' like Émile and Adèle when they spoke in hushed tones about 'Madame'.

Camille bought road maps and they played at travelling across a France unfolded in quarters on the polished ebony table which reflected two upside-down, blurred faces.

They counted the kilometres, disparaged their motor car, cordially insulted each other and felt revived, almost rehabilitated in a forgotten camaraderie. But tropical downpours, with no blustery wind, drowned the last days of June and the terraces of the Quart-de-Brie. Saha, safe behind the closed windows, watched the flat rivulets snaking across the mosaic tiles which Camille mopped by treading towels on them. The horizon, the town, the rain, took on the colour of clouds filled with inexhaustible water.

'Do you want to take the train?' Alain suggested sweetly.

He knew before he said it that Camille would fire up at that detested word. And she did, and swore.

He added: 'I'm afraid you might be bored. All the trips we'd planned...'

'All those summer hotels...All those fly-ridden restaurants...All that sea full of bathers...' she went on plaintively. 'You see, we are used to driving, and that's basically what we know how to do—drive. Not go travelling.'

He saw that she was rather downhearted and gave her a brotherly kiss. But she turned, bit his mouth and earlobe, and they diverted themselves, once more, with the distraction which makes time go quickly and trains the body in the easy attainment of the pleasures of love. It tired Alain. When he dined at his mother's house with Camille and stifled his yawns, Madame Amparat lowered her eyes, and Camille invariably smiled a smug smile. For she noted with some pride the almost aggressive way Alain was beginning to use her, a rapid body-to-body encounter after which, panting, he cast her aside to move over to the cooler side of the uncovered bed.

She joined him there in her innocent fashion, which he didn't forgive her for, although he silently yielded once more. That way he would have the leisure later to seek the source of what he called their incompatibility. He had sense enough not to seek it in their frequent acts of physical possession. Clear-minded, aided by his exhaustion, he climbed back to the refuge where the enmity between a man and a woman is constantly renewed and never grows old. Sometimes she exposed herself to him in a banal place, where she was sleeping innocently in the full sun. And he was stunned, for instance, even scandalized, when he realized how dark Camille was. In bed, lying behind her, he studied the short hairs on the shorn back of her neck, in rows like the prickles on a sea urchin, like hatching on maps of mountains, the shortest of them visible and blue beneath the smooth skin, before each emerged through a small black pore.

'Have I never slept with a brunette before?' he wondered in surprise. 'A couple of little dark girls never made such an impression of brownness on me.' And he held his own arm of a normal yellowy-white up to the light, a blond arm spangled with olive-gold down, irrigated by jade-coloured veins. He compared his own hair to Camille's forest of violet glints, where the strange whiteness of the skin was visible between parallel stems, like fronds of algae, in her abundant, exotic hair.

Seeing one very thin black hair sticking to the rim of the sink made him feel sick. Then this little neurosis changed and moving on from the fine details, he began to criticize her shape. Holding the young body quietly in his arms, her precise contours concealed by the dark, Alain set to blaming a creator, who, as strict as his English nanny of old—'No more prunes than rice, my boy, no more rice than chicken'—had shaped Camille just adequately, and without abundance or imagination. He carried his disapproval, along with his unhappiness, into the antechamber of his dreams, there in the incalculable moment reserved for the land of darkness, peopled by convex eyes, Grecian-nosed sea creatures, moons and chins. There he wished for a backside like those of the nineteenth century, the fullness of it below her unconfined waist to compensate for the sharpness of her small breasts. At other times, half asleep, he compromised, lusting instead after a plentiful bosom, a quivering, double monstrosity of flesh with sensitive tips. Such cravings, born of their lovemaking and outliving it, never saw the light of day or complete wakefulness, but only populated a narrow isthmus between his nightmares and his voluptuous dreams.

Aroused, the stranger smelled of wood gnawed at by flames, she smelled of birch, of violets, she was a whole bouquet of sweet scents, dark and persistent, lingering on the palms of his hands. These fragrances exalted Alain in contradictory ways but did not always arouse his desire.

'You are like the scent of roses,' he said to Camille one day. 'You take away one's appetite.'

She looked at him dubiously, awkward and a little askance, as always when she received a double-edged compliment.

'You sound as if you are back in the 1830s,' she murmured.

'Not as much as you,' replied Alain, 'Definitely not as much as you. I know who you are like.'

'Like Marie Dubas,* I've been told that before.'

'Utterly wrong, my girl! Apart from the braids, you look like every woman weeping at the top of a tower, on the covers of Loïsa Puget's* musical compositions, with your great Greek eyes, your long, thick lashes that make the tears roll down your cheeks...'

One after another Alain's senses deceived him and condemned Camille. But he had to admit that she took it all on the chin, at least,

some of the things he spat at her, words that were not so much grateful as provocative, at the times when, stretched out on the floor, he
weighed her up, looking at her covertly through half-closed eyelids,
and appraised, without particular sympathy or consideration, her
new qualities and especial aptitudes, the rather wearisome but already
cleverly selfish passion of so young a wife. These were moments of
frank clarity, of certainty, during which Camille sought to prolong the
half-silence of their fights, anxious, tense and teetering on the edge.

Having no real malice herself, and partly taken in by his self-
interested provocations, his poignant demands, and even by his new-
found Polynesian cynicism, she did not guess that every time Alain
possessed her, it was for the last time. He was master of her just as if
he had put a hand over her mouth to stop her screaming, or as if he
had beaten her unconscious.

When she was fully dressed again, and sitting up beside him in
their sports car, he could not fathom, could not explain, scrutinizing
her, what had made her into his worst enemy, for as he drew breath
again, as he listened to his heartbeat slowing down, he himself stopped
being the dramatic young man who stripped naked before throwing
his companion to the ground; and the brief voluptuous preliminaries,
the problems of nakedness, the gratitude simulated or real, were rele-
gated to the category of those things that are over and done with and
will probably never return. Then he resumed his main preoccupa-
tion, accepting it as both honourable and natural, the question which
took pride of place because it had merited it for so long: 'How can
I stop Camille living in MY house?'

When the period of hating the 'building works' was over, he had
truly begun to hope for a return to the house of his birth, to the calming arrangement of a life on the soil, dependent always on the earth,
on what the earth brings forth. 'Here I yearn for some fresh air. Oh,'
he sighed, 'to be underneath the trees, to see the birds fly overhead...'
He finished severely: 'But the pastoral life is no solution.' And he had
recourse to his indispensable ally, telling lies.

One afternoon of pure fire that was melting the asphalt, he arrived
at his domain, around which Neuilly was nothing but deserted streets,
empty July trams, dogs yawning in gardens. Before leaving Camille
he had made Saha comfortable on the coolest part of the terrace in the
Quart-de-Brie, vaguely worried as always when he left the two females
alone together.

The house and garden were asleep, and the little iron gate did not creak. Roses that had passed their best, red poppies, the first heliconia with their ruby-red throats, and dark snapdragons were a blaze of colour in the lawn. At the side of the house gaped the new doorway and two more windows in a ground-floor building, freshly painted. 'Everything's finished,' Alain concluded. He walked cautiously, as he did in his dreams, treading only on the grass.

At the murmuring of a voice which rose from the cellar, he stopped, vaguely listening. It was only the familiar old voices, dutiful grumblings—the old voices which used to say 'she' and 'Monsieur Alain' and which flattered the young blond boy, the spindly virile form, his childish spirit...'I was a king,' Alain told himself with a sad smile.

'So *she'll* be coming to sleep here soon?' one of the old voices was clearly heard to say.

'That's Adèle,' Alain said to himself. Propped up against the wall, he listened, without compunction.

'Of course,' Émile was saying, in his quavery voice. 'That apartment's very badly built.'

The maidservant, from the Basque country, going grey and with a beard, interposed:

'I believe you. From their bathroom you can hear everything going on in the lavatory. Monsieur Alain won't like that.'

'*She* said, last time she came, *she* didn't need any curtains in her drawing room, because there aren't any neighbours overlooking the garden.'

'No neighbours? What about us if we go to the wash-house? What'll we see when she's with Monsieur Alain?'

Alain thought he heard stifled laughter as old Émile went on:

'Oh, perhaps we shan't see as much as all that! *She'll* be made to hide herself away too, more often than not...Monsieur Alain's not someone to let himself go like that on any old sofa at all hours of the day and night.'

There was a silence and Alain could hear nothing but the sound of a blade being sharpened on the block. Still he stood listening, leaning against the warm stone wall, vaguely watching out for the moonstone-coloured fur of Saha between a flame-red geranium and the acid-green turf.

Adèle said: 'I find the perfume she wears awful cloying.'

'And her dresses,' chipped in Juliette, the Basque woman, 'what she puts on doesn't look stylish. She looks a bit saucy, more the actressy type. And what's she going to bring with her as lady's maid? Some creature from the orphanage, I daresay, or worse.'

A window was slammed down and the voices were silenced. Alain felt intimidated and rather nervous and was breathing like a man whose life has been spared by murderers. He wasn't surprised, nor was he indignant. Between his own criticism of Camille and the harsh critics in the basement, the difference was not so very great. But his heart was beating fast at having eavesdropped in that underhand fashion, and not paid the penalty, and of assembling the testimony of partisans, of accomplices, without entering into any pact. He mopped his face, took a deep breath as if that blast of unanimous misogyny, that pagan incense offered solely to the male principle, had stunned him. His mother, who, waking from her siesta, was raising the blinds on her room, saw him standing with his cheek still resting against the wall. She shouted softly, like the good mother she was.

'Are you all right, son?'

He caught hold of her hands on the window ledge as though he were her lover.

'I'm fine, Maman. I just walked over...'

'Good idea!'

She didn't think that for a minute, but they smiled at each other, lying, both of them.

'Can I ask you to do something for me, Maman?'

'Something to do with money, I warrant? You're not very well off this year, of course, you poor things...'

'No, Maman. Please would you not tell Camille that I came over today. As I just came for no particular reason, I mean, other than to say hello, I'd rather...And that's not all. I'd like you to give me some advice. Between ourselves, you understand?'

Madame Amparat looked down, ran her hands through her grey wavy hair and tried to ward off his confiding in her.

'I'm not much of a talker, as you know. You've caught me with my hair all over the place. I look like an old gypsy. Won't you come inside where it's cooler?'

'No, Maman. Do you think there's any way—I can't get the thought out of my head—a tactful way, obviously, that would be acceptable to everyone—a way of stopping Camille from living here?'

He squeezed his mother's hands, expecting them to flinch or to pull away. But they remained cold and pliant between his own.

'That's the sort of thing people come out with when they are just married,' she said in some embarrassment.

'What do you mean?'

'With a young married couple it all goes wonderfully well or not at all. And I don't know which is preferable. But it never goes completely smoothly of its own accord.'

'But Maman, that's not what I'm asking you! I'm asking you if there's any way of...'

For the first time he was losing face in front of his mother. She didn't help him, and he turned away petulantly.

'You're talking like a child. You go out in this heat and after you've been quarrelling, you come here and ask me questions...How should I know? Questions that can only be answered by divorce...Or by moving house, or goodness knows what...'

As soon as she started to speak, she struggled for breath and Alain was cross with himself only when he saw how flushed and breathless she'd become after so few words. 'I've said enough for the time being,' he decided prudently.

'We haven't quarrelled, Maman. It's just me, I can't get used to the idea...I shouldn't like to see...'

With an embarrassed wave, he indicated the garden around them, the lake-green lawn, the bed of petals under the rose arbour, the haze of bees above the flowering ivy, the house that was both ugly and revered.

The hand, her sensitive hand that he still held in his, closed into a little fist. Abruptly he kissed it: Enough, enough for today.

'I'm going, Maman. Monsieur Veuillet is going to ring you tomorrow at eight about the share prices going down. Do I look a bit better, Maman?'

He looked up, his eyes green in the shade of the tulip tree, forcing his face, through habit, fondness and diplomacy, into its old childhood expression. He blinked, to make his eyes brighter, flashed her a winning smile and pouted. The maternal hand opened again, passed above the window ledge, reached out to touch Alain on his sensitive, familiar spots, the shoulder blades, the Adam's apple, the top of his arm, and the answer came only after that touching:

'A bit better, yes, you do look a bit better.'

'She was pleased when I asked her not to tell Camille…' When he remembered his mother's final caress, he tightened his belt beneath his jacket. 'I've lost weight. I'm losing weight. No more physical exercise, none except when we make love.'

He went off, light-heartedly, dressed for the season, and felt the fresh breeze drying him, chasing away the acrid scent of his blond sweat, kin to the scent of the black cypress. He was leaving his native stronghold unviolated, his cohort of allies in the basement intact, and the rest of the day would be easy. Until midnight no doubt, beside the inoffensive Camille, he would be sitting in the car, drinking in the evening air, it might be the woodland scent from the oak plantations with their borders of muddy ditches, or the smell of something dry, like a threshing floor. 'And I'll bring back some proper couch-grass for Saha!'

He blamed himself severely for what had happened to his cat, living with so few sounds up on their belvedere. 'She's existing in a sort of chrysalis, and it's all my fault…' When they played their conjugal games, she absented herself so completely that Alain had never seen her in the triangular room. She ate barely enough, no longer communicated in such a variety of ways, nor was so demanding, but preferred her lengthy vigil to anything else. 'She's in that cage all over again, waiting…she's waiting for me.'

Camille's carrying voice came through the closed door as he reached the landing:

'That bloody animal! I wish it would go to hell! What? No, Madame Buque, no matter what you say…I don't give a damn, I tell you.'

He could still hear foul language from her. Very gently he turned the key in the lock, but when he crossed his own threshold, he did not want to listen to her and not be seen. 'What bloody animal? Is there an animal in the house?'

In the flat, Camille, wearing a sleeveless pullover, a knitted beret miraculously balanced on the back of her head, was angrily pulling on her driving gloves and seemed flabbergasted at the sight of her husband.

'It's you! Where've you come from?'

'Nowhere, I'm home. Who are you swearing about?'

With a clever move she averted the question and went on the attack.

'You're being very snappy with me, when you're on time for once. I'm ready, waiting for you!'

'You can't be waiting for me, because I'm on time! Who were you so angry with? I heard you say: "bloody animal". Which animal?'

She looked slightly askance, but her eyes were still fixed on Alain.

'The dog,' she cried. 'That wretched cur downstairs from morning till night! I was shouting at him. Can't you hear him barking? Listen!'

She raised her finger to command his attention and Alain had time to notice that the gloved finger was shaking. He gave in to a naïve need to be reassured.

'For a minute I thought you were speaking about Saha.'

'Me!' cried Camille. 'Talk about Saha like that? Never! It would be more than my life's worth! Now are you coming or not?'

'You get the car out, I'll meet you down there. I'm going to get a handkerchief and a jumper.'

He first looked for the cat, but all he could see on the coolest terrace near the canvas chair that Camille sometimes slept in in the afternoon were some shards of broken glass which he looked at dumbly.

'The cat's down here with me, Monsieur,' came the reedy voice of Madame Buque. 'She likes my stool with the wicker seat, she sharpens her claws on it.'

'In the kitchen!' Alain thought sadly. 'My little puma, my garden cat, my cat of the lilac and maybugs—in the kitchen! Oh, it's all got to change!'

He gave Saha a kiss on her forehead, muttered some little ritual verses to her and promised her couch-grass and the flowers of the sweet acacia. But he thought the cat and Madame Buque didn't really look right, Madame Buque especially.

'We may be back for dinner, or we may not, Madame Buque. Has the cat got everything she needs?'

'Yes, yes, Monsieur,' Madame Buque said hastily. 'Monsieur knows I do all I can…'

The matronly figure was red in the face and seemed on the verge of tears. She stroked the cat's back in a kindly, unpractised way. Saha arched her back and uttered a tiny mew like that of some timid and pathetic creature and it broke her friend's heart.

The drive was better than he expected. Sitting at the wheel, alert and with hand and foot finely coordinated, Camille drove him to the hills at Montfort-l'Amaury.

'Shall we have supper outside, Alain? Darling?

She was smiling at him in profile, beautiful as she always was in the dusk, her cheek brown and transparent, the corner of her eye and her teeth the same dazzling white. In the forest of Rambouillet she put down the windscreen and the wind filled Alain's ears with the sound of trees and running water.

'A little rabbit!' Camille cried. 'A pheasant!'

'It's still a rabbit! One moment more and...'

'That one doesn't know how lucky he was!'

'You've got a dimple in your cheek like in your photos as a child,' Alain said, more animated now.

'Don't speak of it, I'm getting so fat!' she replied, shaking her shoulders.

He waited for her to smile and show the dimple again, and let his eyes fall on her strong neck, with no sign of the 'necklace of Venus', a firm round neck like that of a beautiful white negress. 'Yes, she's put on weight...And in the most attractive way...Her breasts too...' He turned back to himself and morosely came up against the age-old male complaint: 'She's put on weight because we make love...because of me.' He slid a jealous hand under his jacket, felt his ribs, and ceased to admire the childish dimple and cheeks.

But his pride was evident when he sat down a little later at the table of a famous restaurant where the diners at the neighbouring table stopped speaking and eating to look at Camille. And he exchanged a smile with his wife, with a movement of the chin, the coquettish rituals appropriate for a 'handsome couple'.

And anyway, it was for him alone, and not to show off, that Camille's voice grew huskier, and she became rather charmingly languorous. For his part Alain quickly took the hors d'œuvre plate of tomatoes and the basket of strawberries from her, insisted she help herself to creamed chicken and poured out her wine, which she didn't much like, but drank rapidly.

'I'm not fond of wine, as you know,' she repeated each time she emptied her glass.

The almost white light in the sky was not borne away by the setting sun, and there were still little scraps of cloud of a dark rose hue. But from the forest, looming massively behind the tables outside the inn, the night and the cold seemed to be emerging. Camille put her hand on Alain's.

'What? What? What is it?' he cried in terror.

Astonished, she took away her hand. The small amount of wine she had drunk lit up her moist eyes, in which the pink bobbing globes swinging on the pergola were reflected in miniature.

'Nothing, for goodness' sake! You're nervous as a cat...Am I not allowed to put my hand on yours?'

'I thought,' he admitted weakly, 'I thought you wanted to tell me something, something serious...I thought', he blurted out, 'you were going to tell me you're pregnant.'

Camille's small high-pitched laugh drew the attention of the men still at nearby tables.

'And are you so overwhelmed? With joy...or annoyance?'

'I don't really know...What about you? How would you feel? Happy or unhappy? We haven't thought about it very much, well I haven't anyway...Why are you laughing?'

'Your face...Suddenly you look like a man going to the gallows... It's very funny. I'll have to unstick my eyelashes.'

With her two index fingers she lifted the lashes of both eyes.

'It's not funny, it's serious,' Alain said, relieved he could cover up his true feelings. 'But why am I so scared?' he thought to himself.

'It's only serious for people who don't have anywhere to live, or who only have a small apartment. But we...'

Quite at ease, with the treacherous wine rendering her poised and optimistic, she was smoking and talking as though to herself, her thighs against the table and her legs crossed.

'Pull your skirt down, Camille.'

She didn't hear, and went on:

'We've got everything you need for a baby: a garden—what a garden! And a dream bedroom with its own bathroom.'

'A bedroom?'

'Your old bedroom we're having redecorated. And please don't insist on a frieze of small ducks and Vosges pine trees with a sky in the background...That would set a bad example for our progeny in matters of taste...'

He was careful not to stop her. Her cheeks aflame, she talked easily, dwelling on the distant plans she was forming in her mind. He had never seen her look more beautiful. He was struck by the base of her neck, like a slender, unblemished tree-trunk, an enfolded cluster of muscles, and on her nostrils blowing out smoke. 'When I give her pleasure and she purses her mouth, she widens her nostrils to breathe, like a little pony.'

He heard the rouged, disdainful lips utter predictions that were so outrageous they did not startle him anymore: Camille the woman was calmly moving forward among the wreck of Alain's past. 'The little minx,' he thought, 'she's organized everything...Now I'm learning!' Later there would be a tennis court on the big useless lawn. The kitchen and the pantry...'

'Have you never realized how inconvenient they are, what a waste of space? Like the garage...All I am telling you, darling, is so you know that I'm thinking a lot about when we move in properly. But above all else we must handle your mother, who is so kind, and we must never do anything without her agreement, must we?'

He said yes and no haphazardly as he gathered together the wild strawberries scattered over the tablecloth. A temporary rest, a fore-taste of indifference after she said 'your old bedroom' had rendered him numb.

'There's only one thing that might make it more urgent for us,' she continued. 'Patrick's last postcard was dated from the Balearics, mind you...it'll take less time for Patrick to come back from the Balearics if he doesn't stay lying around on the beaches, than for our decorator to finish everything—I hope he'll come to a sticky end, that son of Penelope and a tortoise!* But I shall sing my siren song: "Patrick, darling", and you know that Patrick is very affected by my siren voice...'

'The Balearics...' Alain broke in, thinking. 'The Balearic islands.'

'It's next door, so to speak...Where are you going? Are we leaving? It was so nice here.'

Standing up, now sober, she was yawning with tiredness and shivering.

'I'll drive,' said Alain. 'Put on the old coat under the cushion. And have a sleep.'

A volley of mayflies, quicksilver moths, stag beetles hard as pebbles whirled towards them in the headlights and the motor car forced back the rush of wings like a wave. Camille did indeed fall asleep, sitting upright, trained not to lean on the shoulder and arm of the driver even when she slept. All she did was acknowledge with little jerks of her head the jolts in the road.

'From the Balearics,' Alain mused. Thanks to the night air and the white headlights which caught, rebuffed, decimated the flying crea-tures, he reinstated the overpopulous vestibule of his dreams, the dusty firmament of exploding faces, large hostile eyes which put off to the next day a reckoning, a password, a number. So much so that he forgot to take the shortest way between Pontchartrain and the octroi in Versailles, and Camille groaned in her sleep. 'Bravo,' Alain applauded. 'A good reaction! Good little faithful, watchful senses... Oh how I like you and how easily we get on when you are asleep and I'm awake.'

Their bare heads and their sleeves were wet with dew when they set foot again in their new street, deserted in the moonlight. Alain looked up: in the middle of the almost round moon, just above the nine storeys a little horned shadow of a cat leaned over, waiting. He pointed her out to Camille:

'Look at her, waiting!'

'You must have good eyesight,' said Camille with a yawn.

'Supposing she fell! Don't call her, whatever you do!'

'You needn't worry,' Camille said. 'If I called her, she wouldn't come.'

'I'm not surprised,' Alain laughed unkindly.

As soon as he spoke, he could have bitten his tongue. 'Too hasty! Too hasty! And what a time to choose!' Camille's hand reaching for the doorbell did not make it.

'Not surprised? What do you mean? Go on, say it! Have I once again not treated the unmentionable animal with respect? Has the cat been complaining?'

'No progress there then,' thought Alain as he shut the garage door. He crossed the road again and rejoined his wife who was waiting for him in attack mode. 'Either I say sorry and we have a quiet night—or we come to blows and there's no more argument...Or...I've been too hasty.'

'Well, I've something to say to you!'

'Let's go up first!' said Alain.

They were silent in the tiny lift, squashed against one another. As soon as they reached the flat Camille threw her beret and gloves down as though to indicate she wasn't abandoning their quarrel. Alain was busying himself with Saha, trying to get her to leave her perilous perch. Patiently, anxious not to displease, the cat followed him into the bathroom.

'If it's because of what you heard before dinner when you got back...', Camille began sharply as soon as he reappeared.

Alain had made up his mind and interrupted her with a weary air: 'My dear girl, what can we say to one another? Nothing we don't know already. That you don't like the cat, that you told Madame Buque off because the cat broke a vase—or a glass, I saw the pieces? I shall reply that I love Saha, that your jealousy would be more or less the same if I had retained a warm affection for a childhood friend. And the night would be spent like that. No, thank you very much. I prefer to sleep. Well, next time I advise you to take the initiative and get a little dog.'

Camille stopped short, eyebrows raised, not knowing where to direct her anger.

'Next time? What next time? What do you mean? What initiative?'

As Alain shrugged, she flushed and her face crumpled like a child, her eyes grew very bright with unshed tears:

'Oh,' groaned Alain inwardly, 'I'm sick of this. She's going to tell me I'm right. She's going to give in. I'm sick of this.'

'Listen, Alain.'

With an effort he feigned anger, made a pretence of having some authority.

'No, my dear, no, no! You won't make me end this evening, which was delightful, with a useless argument! No, you won't turn what is a childish dispute into a tragedy, any more than you will prevent me from loving animals!'

A sort of bitter gaiety came into Camille's eyes, but she said nothing. 'Perhaps I went a bit far. Childish was too much. And as for loving animals, what do I know?'

A small shape, a blue shadow, encircled like a cloud with a hem of silver, sitting on the vertiginous border of the night, occupied his thoughts and took him away from the soulless place where step by step he stood up for his chance of solitude, his egotism, his poetry...

'Come on, my little enemy,' he said with a false charm, 'let's go to bed.'

She opened the bathroom door where Saha, settled down for the night on the sponge-topped stool, seemed to pay her the bare minimum of attention.

'But why, I don't understand...Why did you say: next time?'

The noise of the water drowned out Camille's voice and Alain no longer spoke. When he went back to her in the large bed, he wished her goodnight and kissed her briefly on her powderless nose, while Camille's mouth kissed his chin with an eager little sound.

Waking early, he slipped quietly off to lie down again on the 'waiting-room bench', on the narrow couch squashed in between two glass partitions.

That's where he went on succeeding nights to finish his sleep. He closed the thick waxed curtains on either side, they were almost new but already much damaged by the sunlight. He could smell on his body the very aroma of solitude, the acrid feline smell of rest-harrow and the flowering box shrub. One arm stretched out, the other folded under his chest, he resumed the limp, independent position he used to sleep in when he was a child. Suspended at the narrow top of the triangular building, he tried, as hard as he could, to summon up the return of his old dreams which had disintegrated in the fatigue of lovemaking.

He escaped more easily than Camille would have wanted, there perforce in their apartment, just vanishing, since escape no longer meant creeping downstairs, slamming the taxi door, the brief note... No mistress had given him an inkling of what Camille would be like, of Camille's easy youthfulness and incalculable appetite, nor of Camille with her sense of honour as the offended party.

Having escaped, lying down again on the 'waiting-room bench' and feeling with the back of his neck for a little rolled-up cushion that he liked more than any other, Alain anxiously listened for a sound from the bedroom he had just left. But Camille didn't open the door again. Alone, she pulled the crumpled sheet over her and the silk eiderdown, bit her bent index finger in mortification and regret, and with a quick tap lowered the long eyebrow of chrome metal which projected a narrow bridge of white light across the bed. Alain never knew if she had slept in the empty bed where she was learning at such a young age that a solitary night necessitates an armed awakening, for she reappeared rested, with only a little make-up, abandoning her bathrobe and pyjamas of the night before. But she couldn't understand that the sensual humour of the male lasts but a brief season, and that its uncertain return is never a new beginning.

Lying there alone, bathed in the night air, measuring the silence and height of his tower by the faint sounds of the boats on the nearby Seine, Alain deliberately delayed falling asleep till Saha appeared. She came to find him, a shadow bluer than shadow, on the ledge of the open window. She stayed there watching and didn't jump down on to Alain's chest, even though he was cajoling her with words she recognized.

'Come my little puma, come here...My cat of the mountains, my
cat of the lilacs, Saha, Saha, Saha...'

She resisted, sitting above him on the window ledge. All he could
see was her cat-shape against the sky, her chin tilted, her ears pointed
passionately towards him, and he could never catch the expression in
her eyes.

Sometimes the dry dawn, the dawn before the wind got up, saw
them sitting on the east terrace, contemplating cheek to cheek the
paling of the sky and the white pigeons taking off one by one from the
beautiful cedar tree at the Folie-Saint-James.* They were both surprised to be so far above the earth, so alone and so unhappy. Making
the passionate and undulating movement of a hunting creature, Saha
watched the flight of the pigeons and under her breath uttered a few
'ek...ek' sounds, the feeble echo of the 'mouek...mouek' she uttered
when excited, covetous, or when playing a violent game.

'*Our* room,' Alain whispered to her. 'Our garden, our house.'

She was getting thinner again, and Alain was delighted by her slender form. But he couldn't bear to see her so placid and patient, like all
those who are kept alive, but worn-out by a distant promise.

Sleep gradually overcame Alain as the opening day shortened the
shadows. Without a crown at first and looking bigger through the
haze of Paris, then smaller, lighter and already scorching, the sun
rose, casting its light over the chattering sparrows in the gardens. On
the terraces, on the rails of balconies, in small courtyards where captive bushes longed for water, the strengthening daylight revealed the
disorder of a warm night, an item of clothing left on a long rattan
seat, empty glasses on a small iron table, a pair of sandals. Alain hated
the shamelessness of these little apartments oppressed by the summer, and swiftly he returned to bed through an open window in the
partition. At the bottom of this nine-storey house in a little garden of
spindly vegetables, a gardener looked up to see that young man in
white, like a burglar, step through the transparent partition.

Saha didn't follow. Now and then she pricked up an ear in the
direction of the triangular room, now she noted, without much interest, the waking of a distant world down on the ground. A dog let out
from a small, dilapidated house raced silently round and round the
small garden and only recovered his voice after a pointless chase.
Women appeared at the windows, a furious servant slammed doors,
shook out orange cushions on a flat roof like those in Italy, men

dragged themselves from their sleep and lit up the first bitter-tasting cigarette. Finally, in that kitchen in the Quart-de-Brie where no fire was ever lit, came the discordant whistling of the automatic coffee machine and the electric tea-kettle; through the glass door of the bathroom drifted Camille's scent and her noisy yawn. Saha, resigned, tucked her paws back under her stomach and pretended to sleep.

8

ONE July evening while they were both waiting for Alain to come home, Camille and the cat were relaxing on the same parapet, the cat lying with her paws tucked under her, Camille leaning on it with her arms folded. Camille did not care much for this balcony-terrace, which was reserved for the cat, with two stone walls protecting it from the wind and from all communication with the terrace at the prow of the building.

They exchanged a purely exploratory glance, and Camille did not speak to Saha. Leaning over as if to count the rows of orange shutters festooning the vertiginous façade from top to bottom, she brushed against the cat, who got up to give her more room, stretched, and lay down again a little way off.

As soon as Camille was left alone, she strongly resembled the little girl who refused to say hello, and her face took on that childlike expression of inhuman naïvety and angelic obstinacy that ennobles the faces of children. She cast an indifferent, unsympathetic, though possibly not critical, glance over Paris and over the sky from which the light departed earlier each day. She yawned nervously, drew herself up, took a few distracted steps, and leaned out again, obliging the cat to jump down. Saha withdrew in a dignified fashion and tried to go back into the bedroom. But the door of the hypotenuse was shut and Saha sat down patiently. One moment later she had to get out of Camille's way as she paced from one wall to the other with long, energetic strides, and the cat jumped up on to the parapet. As if in play, Camille leaned out and dislodged her, and Saha went to sit outside the closed door again.

With a far-off look in her eye, Camille stood still with her back to her. Yet the cat watched Camille's back and her breathing got quicker. She got up, turned round two or three times, studied the closed door. Camille had not moved. Saha's nostrils swelled, she looked anxious and sickly; a long, pathetic mew, an answer to an imminent, unspoken threat escaped her, and Camille turned round abruptly.

She was slightly pale, that is to say her make-up described two oval moons on her cheeks. She assumed an absent-minded air, as she would have done had a person been looking at her. She even began humming a little tune between her closed lips and began walking again from one wall to the other, keeping time with the rhythm of her song, but her voice failed. She forced the cat, whom her foot was about to kick, first to jump up on to her narrow viewing ledge and then to crouch against the door.

Saha had recovered her composure and would have died rather than utter another cry. Following the cat, but appearing not to see her, Camille paced back and forth in complete silence. Saha only leaped on to the parapet when she felt Camille's feet on top of her, and jumped down on to the floor of the balcony in order to avoid the outstretched arm which would have hurled her from the height of the nine storeys.

She fled systematically, leapt up carefully, kept her eyes fixed on her adversary, and did not demean herself by either anger or supplication. Extreme emotion, fear of dying, moistened the sensitive soles of her paws, which made marks like flowers on the stucco floor.

Camille seemed the first to weaken, her criminal strength dissolving. She made the mistake of noticing that the sun would soon be gone, gave a swift glance at her wristwatch, heard the tinkle of glasses in the apartment. Another moment or two and her resolve, abandoning her, just as sleep abandons the sleepwalker, would leave her guiltless but exhausted. Saha felt her enemy's resolve weaken, and hesitated on the parapet as Camille, with both arms, pushed her out into the void.

She had time to hear the claws scrape on the balcony's rough facing, to see Saha's blue body twisted in an S-shape, clinging on to thin air with all the force of a trout rising to the surface, then she drew back against the wall.

She had no inclination to look down, into the little kitchen garden surrounded by rubble. Back in the room she placed her hands over her ears, then took them away and shook her head as though she could hear the buzzing of a mosquito, sat down and almost fell asleep; but the approaching night set her once more on her feet and she dispelled the twilight by lighting the glass bricks, the luminous strips, the glaring mushroom lamps, as well as the long eyebrow of chrome which beamed its opaline eye across the bed.

She moved with a sort of buoyancy, touching various objects with light, skilful, dreaming hands.

'It's as if I've lost weight,' she said aloud.

She changed into some white clothes.

'My little fly in milk,' she said, imitating Alain's voice.

Her cheeks regained their colour as a carnal memory went through her head and brought her back to the present, as she waited for Alain to arrive.

She listened out for the hum of the lift, she shuddered at every sound, the thudding, like a springboard; the metallic clangs; the grinding of a boat on its moorings, a muffled music—sounds of the discordant life of a new house. But she wasn't surprised when the buzz of the bell in the hall succeeded the sound of a key in the lock. She ran to open it herself.

'Shut the door!', Alain ordered. 'First, I've got to see she's not hurt. Come over here and give me some light.'

He carried Saha, alive, in his arms. He went straight into the bedroom, pushed aside the ornaments on the invisible dressing table and put the cat down gently on the glass surface. She remained upright and steady on her legs but looked around her with deep-set eyes, exactly as she would have done in unfamiliar surroundings.

'Saha!' Alain spoke gently to her. 'If she's not hurt, it'll be a miracle... Saha!'

She raised her head as if to reassure her friend and her cheek brushed against his hand.

'Walk a little, Saha...She's walking! Unbelievable, she fell six floors. It was that chap's awning on the second floor that broke her fall. Then she rebounded from there on to the concierge's bit of lawn, he saw her whizz past. He said: "I thought it was an umbrella falling." What's wrong with her ear? No, it's only the white stuff from the wall. Wait while I listen to her heart.'

He laid the cat on her side and felt her ribs thumping, her body's tiny engine so disturbed. His blond hair falling over his face, his eyes shut, he seemed to be asleep against Saha's side, then waking with a sigh, only to see Camille standing there, silently looking at the picture they made, the two of them.

'Can you believe it, she's not hurt! At least I can't find anything, except her heart's thumping really fast, though a cat's heart normally beats fast. But how on earth can it have happened? I'm asking you as if you could possibly know, my love. She fell from this side,' he said, looking at the open glass door...'Jump down Saha, if you can.'

After some hesitation she jumped down but settled again on the rug. Her breath came and went swiftly and she went on looking uncertainly all round the bedroom.

'I feel like phoning Chéron...But she's washing herself, look! She wouldn't lick herself if there was something wrong inside... Oh God!'

He stretched, threw his jacket on to the bed and came over to Camille.

'What a fright! How pretty you are, all in white. Kiss me, my little fly in milk!'

She surrendered to his arms, which at last remembered her, and she could not hold back her sobs.

'Oh no, are you crying?'

He was also distressed, hid his forehead in the soft, black hair.

'I...I didn't know you cared about her...'

She had the courage not to free herself from his clasp when he said that. In any case Alain returned immediately to Saha, wanting to take her on to the terrace because of the heat. But the cat resisted, preferring to lie down near the door, facing the blue evening sky, her own colour. From time to time she gave a little shiver and surveyed the depths of the triangular room behind her.

'It's the shock,' Alain explained. 'I would have liked to take her out in the fresh air.'

'Leave her,' Camille said weakly, 'since she doesn't want to go.'

'Her wish is our command. Especially today! What is there left that's eatable at this time of day? Nine-thirty!'

Mother Buque wheeled the table out on to the terrace, and they dined facing east, the area of Paris the most dotted with lights. Alain chattered on, drank wine diluted with water, accused Saha of being clumsy, of not being careful enough, called it 'a cat's sin'.

'*Cat's sins* are sorts of sporting errors, weaknesses attributable to their having been civilized and domesticated. They've nothing in common with clumsiness, sudden movements that are almost deliberate...'

But this time Camille did not ask him: 'How do you know that?'

After dinner, taking Camille with him, he carried Saha off into the living room, where the cat consented to drink the milk she had refused earlier. As she drank, she started to shake all over, like a cat given water that's too cold.

'The shock,' Alain repeated. 'All the same I'll ask Chéron to come and check her out tomorrow morning...Oh, I'm forgetting everything!' he cried gaily. 'Phone the concierge! I left the roll of plans our blessed furniture man Massart delivered in the lodge.'

Camille did as she was told, while Alain, tired, relaxed, collapsed into one of the armchairs and closed his eyes:

'Hello!' Camille phoned. 'Yes, that must be it...A large roll... Thank you very much.'

He was laughing, with his eyes still closed. She had come back to stand by him and watched him laughing.

'What a tiny voice you've got! What's this new little voice all about? "A large roll...thank you very much," he mimicked. 'Are you saving such a tiny voice for the concierge? Come on, between the two of us we'll confront the latest creations of Massart!'

He unrolled a long strip of Whatmann paper* on the ebony table. Immediately Saha, loving any kind of paper, jumped up on to the design.

'Oh, what a nice little cat!' Alain exclaimed. 'That's to show me she's not hurt. My escaped puss! Has she got a bump on her head? Camille, feel her head. No, she hasn't got a bump. Feel her head anyway, Camille.'

An obedient little assassin, trying to find a way out of the depths of banishment, stretched out her hand and lightly and humbly touched the detested cat's head.

The most savage yowling and growling followed by a mad leap in the air was the cat's reaction, and Camille shouted 'Aah!' as if she had been burned. Standing on the unrolled wallpaper, the cat bared her teeth, revealing the dry redness of her throat, her hackles raised, heaping passionate accusations upon the young woman.

Alain stood up, ready to protect Saha and Camille from one another.

'Careful! Perhaps she's gone mad! Saha...'

She stared angrily at him, but lucidly, which attested to her soundness of mind.

'What happened? Where did you touch her?'

'I didn't touch her.'

They were speaking softly to one another, scarcely moving their lips.

'Well, it's very odd,' Alain said. 'I don't understand it. Put your hand out again.'

'No, I'm not going to,' protested Camille. 'Perhaps she's got rabies,' she added.

Alain risked stroking Saha, whose hackles subsided as she moulded herself into her friend's palm, but brought her shining eyes back to rest on Camille.

'Well, it's very odd!' Alain said again slowly. 'Oh, look she's got a scratch on her nose. I didn't see that. It's dried blood. Saha, Saha, good girl...' he said as he saw the fury increase in her yellow eyes.

The furious cat's puffed-out cheeks and her whiskers pointing straight in front of her made it look as if she were laughing. The thrill of the fight pulled down the purple corners of her mouth, tensed the muscles in her mobile chin, and her entire feline face forced itself into a universal language, into some word that humans have forgotten.

'What's that?' Alain suddenly asked.

'What's what?'

Beneath the cat's gaze, Camille was recovering her courage and her instinct of self-defence. Bent over the design, Alain was puzzling about the wet footmarks, in groups of four little marks around a central irregular mark.

'Her paws...all damp?' Alain murmured.

'She must have trodden in some water,' said Camille. 'You make up stories out of nothing!'

Alain looked up at the blue, rainless night.

'In water? What water?'

With widening eyes, looking strangely ugly, he turned to his wife.

'Don't you know what those marks are?' he said sharply. 'No, you don't. It's fear, do you understand? Fear. The cat's sweat, the cat's sweat, the only reason cats ever sweat. So, she must have been frightened by something.'

He gently took one of Saha's front paws and dried the fleshy pad with his finger. Then he folded back the living white sheath which concealed her retractile nails:

'All her claws are broken...' he said, talking to himself. 'She's clung on, she's clawed at the stone as she tried to cling to it...She...'

He broke off and without another word, took the cat under his arm into the bathroom.

Alone, motionless, Camille listened. Her hands were knotted tightly and, though free, they seemed fettered.

'Have you any milk, Madame Buque?' said Alain's voice.

'Yes, Monsieur, in the refrigerator.'

'So is it very cold?'

'I can warm it on the ring…It won't take a second. Is it for the cat? She isn't ill, is she?'

'No, she's…'

Alain's voice stopped abruptly and altered:

'…She's off her meat this hot weather…Thank you, Madame Buque. Yes, you can go. See you tomorrow morning.'

Camille heard her husband walk back and forth and turn on a tap, and knew he was giving the cat food and water. A diffused shadow above the metal lampshade crept up her face where only her large eyes slowly moved.

Alain came back, casually tightening his leather belt, and sat down at the ebony table. But he didn't ask Camille to come back and sit beside him and she was obliged to speak first.

'Did you send Madame Buque home?'

'Yes, should I not have done?'

He lit a cigarette, squinting over the flame of the lighter.

'I wanted her to bring me something tomorrow morning…Oh it's not important, don't apologize.'

'I'm not apologizing. I suppose I should have.'

He went over to the open French windows, drawn by the blue night sky. He was aware of himself trembling, not because of the recent excitement, the tremor was more like the subdued tremolo in an orchestra, heralding the beginning of a piece of music. A rocket went up from the Folie-Saint-James and burst into petals of light, which withered one by one as they fell, and the hazy blue deep of the night took back its quiet. In the Folie park a rockery grotto, a row of pillars, and a fountain lit up in luminescent white and Camille drew nearer to him.

'Are they celebrating something? Let's wait for the fireworks. Can you hear the guitars?'

He didn't answer, too concerned with his own trembling. His wrists and hands tingled, his tired back pained him all over and, acutely, he felt the detested weariness, the fatigue of past sports competitions at school—running, rowing—from which he used to emerge in a vindictive frame of mind, shaking and exhausted, despising equally his victory or his defeat. He was only calm in that part of himself that no longer worried about Saha. For some time, or for a very short while after he had discovered her broken claws, ever since Saha's furious display of fear, he had not really been aware of time. 'It's not fireworks,' he said. 'Dancing, more like.'

From the movement that Camille made next to him in the shadows he realized she was not expecting him to answer. But she plucked up her courage and drew nearer again. He felt she was approaching without apprehension, saw out of the corner of his eye the white dress, the naked arm, half of her face lit up yellow in the room's lamps, half of it blue, absorbed by the clear night, two halves divided by the regular little nose, each endowed with a large eye that scarcely blinked.

'Yes, dancing,' she said approvingly. 'They're mandolins, not guitars...Listen...*Les donneurs...de sé-é-réna...des, Et les bel-les é-écouteu...*'*

On the high note her voice faltered, and she coughed, to excuse her failure.

'But what a strange little voice...' Alain was surprised. 'What's happened to her voice, so loud and open like her eyes? She's singing like a little girl, and she's getting hoarse.'

The mandolins fell silent, the breeze carried over a distant human sound of pleasure and applause. Soon afterwards a rocket went up, exploded in a canopy of purple sparks from which hung teardrops of living fire.

'Oh!' cried Camille.

Like two statues they surged out of the shadow, Camille made of lilac-coloured marble, Alain whiter, with greenish hair and bleached eyes. Once the rocket had gone out, Camille sighed.

'Always too quick,' she said plaintively.

The distant music began again. But a whim of the wind distorted the sound of the high-pitched instruments and the loud, strong tempo of one of the accompanying brass instruments on two notes rose heavily up to where they sat.

'It's a pity,' said Camille. 'They've got the best jazz band without a doubt. They are playing *Love in the Night*...

She hummed the tune in an indescribable voice, high and quavery, as though she had just been crying. This new tone made Alain doubly uneasy, produced in him a need for revelation, the desire to break down whatever it was that—for a long, or perhaps very short, time—was coming between Camille and himself and which he could not yet name but was growing fast, and prevented him from putting his arm round Camille's neck in a comradely fashion; it kept him standing motionless and alert at her side, against the wall that was still warm from the heat of the day. He grew impatient and said:

'Carry on singing…'

A long shower of blue, white, and red scored the heavens over the park, branching out like weeping willows, and revealed to Alain a Camille surprised and already mistrustful.

'Singing what?'

'*Love in the Night* or anything you like…'

She hesitated, refused:

'Let me listen to the jazz…Even from this high up you can hear that it's incredibly accomplished…'

He did not insist, contained his impatience, managed to control the tingling over his whole body.

A swarm of pretty little suns shot into the sky, revolving lightly in the night, while Alain secretly compared them with the constellations of his favourite dreams.

'I must hang on to those, I'll try to take them with me down there,' he noted gravely. 'I've been badly neglecting my dreams.' At last in the sky above the Folie a sort of drifting aurora, yellow and pink, rose up, swelled and exploded into vermilion jewels, fiery ferns, and dazzling ribbons of metal.

Children's shouts on the terraces below greeted the miracle, by the light of which Alain saw that Camille was preoccupied, absorbed, repossessed by other flashes of light…

As soon as the night came down, he hesitated no longer and slipped his bare arm into Camille's. As he touched it, it seemed to him that it was white, scarcely browned by the summer sun, clothed in a fine down covering the skin, bronze on her forearm, paler near her shoulder.

'You're cold…' he murmured. 'Are you poorly?'

She sobbed softly, so much on cue that Alain suspected she had prepared her tears.

'No, it's you,' she said. 'You…you don't love me.'

He stood with his back against the wall and pressed Camille against his hip. He felt her trembling and cold from her shoulder to her knees, bare above her rolled stockings. She clung to him and did not move away.

'Ah! So I don't love you. All right. Is this another jealous scene because of Saha?'

Throughout her body resting against him he could feel a rippling of muscle, a recovery of defensive energy, the whole weight of her body on him and, encouraged by the lateness of the hour, by an indefinable urge to seize the moment, he insisted:

'Instead of adopting this lovely animal, like me…Are we the only couple bringing up a cat or a dog? Would you like to have a parrot, a marmoset, a pair of doves or a dog, and make me very jealous as well?'

She shook her shoulders, in sorrowful and mute objection. Alain straightened up, carefully modulated his voice and spurred himself on: 'Come on, come on, pad it out with a few stupidities and we might be getting somewhere. She's like an earthenware jar I have to tip up and empty…Come on, come on…'

'Would you like a little lion, a baby crocodile scarcely fifty years old? No? Come on now, you'd do better to adopt Saha…If you could be bothered, you'd soon see…'

Camille tore herself away from his grasp so violently, he nearly fell over.

'No,' she cried. 'Never! Do you hear me? Never!'

She let out a furious sigh and repeated not so loudly:

'Oh no, never!'

'That's it,' thought Alain, savouring the moment.

He pushed Camille into the bedroom, let down the external shutters, turned on the rectangle lamp on the ceiling and shut the window. Like an animal, Camille moved nearer the door, which Alain opened again:

'On condition you don't scream,' he said.

He wheeled the only armchair towards Camille and sat astride the solitary chair at the bottom of the wide bed, turned down with its clean sheets. The oilcloth curtain, drawn across ready for the night, tinged Camille's pale face and her crumpled white dress a greenish colour.

'So?' Alain began. 'Impossible? A dreadful state of affairs? You or her?'

She replied by a brief nod, and Alain realized he would have to abandon his bantering tone.

'What do you want me to say?' he went on after a silence. 'The only thing I don't want to say? You know very well I shan't give this cat up. I should be ashamed. Ashamed for myself and for her.'

'I know,' said Camille.

'And ashamed for you,' Alain finished.

'Oh, *me*,' said Camille, with a wave.

'You count too,' Alain said firmly. 'Let's get it clear, is it just me you have a grudge against? You don't blame Saha for anything except being fond of me?'

A sad, hesitant look was her only answer and he was annoyed by having to ask her more questions. He had thought that a short, violent showdown would force all issues, he had relied on that. But after the first protest, Camille retreated into herself and did not add fuel to the fire. He tried being patient.

'Tell me, my love...What? Can't I call you *love*? Tell me, if another cat, not Saha, was involved, would you be more tolerant?'

'Of course,' she answered, very quickly. 'You wouldn't love her like you do that one.'

'That's true, 'said Alain with a considered loyalty.

'Even a woman,' Camille continued, getting heated, 'even a woman, you probably wouldn't love her as much.'

'That's true,' Alain agreed.

'You're not like other animal-lovers...Patrick loves animals, he takes hold of dogs by the scruff of the neck, he rolls them over, he imitates cats to see what they will do, he whistles at birds...'

'Yes, he's a simple soul,' said Alain.

'You are different, you love Saha.'

'I never pretended otherwise, but I didn't lie to you when I said: "Saha's not your rival."'

He broke off and lowered his eyes, guarding his secret, a secret about purity.

'There are rivals *and* rivals,' Camille said sarcastically.

She suddenly went red, flared up in an abrupt fit of outrage and went on the attack.

'I've seen you!' she cried. 'In the mornings when you spend the night on the small divan, before dawn, I've seen the pair of you.'

Her hand trembling, she pointed towards the terrace.

'Both sitting there...You didn't even hear me! You were like this, cheek to cheek.'

She went to the window, took a deep breath and came back to Alain.

'You're the one to say honestly if I'm wrong to hold a grudge against this cat and if I'm wrong to suffer like this.'

He was silent for such a long time she got annoyed again.

'Well speak! Say something! Now we've got this far. What are you waiting for?'

'What you'll say next,' Alain said. 'The rest.'

He got up quietly, leaned over his wife, and lowering his voice, pointed to the French window.

'You did it, didn't you? You threw her over?'

Moving swiftly, she put the bed between herself and him but did not deny it. He looked at her trying to get away from him with a sort of smile.

'So, you threw her over,' he mused. 'I felt that you had changed everything between us, you threw her over. She broke her claws trying to cling on to the wall.'

He lowered his eyes, imagining the murder attempt.

'But how did you do it? Holding her by the scruff of the neck? Taking advantage of her sleeping on the parapet? Had you been preparing your attack for a long time? Was there a struggle before…?'

He looked up again, studied Camille's hands and arms.

'No, you don't have any marks. But she properly laid the blame on you, didn't she, when I forced you to touch her? She was magnificent.'

His eyes left Camille and encompassed the night, the embers of the stars, the tops of the three poplar trees lit up by the lights in the bedroom.

'Well,' he said simply. 'I'm leaving.'

'Oh listen, listen to me,' Camille pleaded in panic, in a very low voice.

But she let him leave the bedroom. He opened the cupboards, talked to the cat in the bathroom. The sound of his footsteps alerted Camille that he had just put on his town shoes, and she automatically checked the time. He came back, carrying Saha in the round wicker basket that Madame Buque used for doing the shopping. Dressed in a hurry, his hair uncombed, a scarf round his neck, he had an air of a lover in disarray, and Camille's eyelids swelled. But she heard Saha moving around in the basket and pursed her lips.

'So, I'm going,' Alain said again.

He lowered his eyes, lifted the basket a little and corrected himself, with studied cruelty:

'*We're* going.'

He secured the wicker lid of the basket, explaining:

'That's all I could find in the kitchen.'

'Are you going home?' Camille asked, forcing herself to copy Alain's air of calm.

'Of course.'

'Are you…Can I expect to see you one day soon?'

'Certainly.'

Surprised, she melted again, stopping herself from pleading, from weeping, with an effort.

'What about you?' Alain said. 'Are you staying here on your own tonight? You won't be scared? If you were to insist, I would stay, but…'

He looked at the terrace:

'But to be quite honest, I don't really want to. What are you going to tell them at home?'

Hurt that, with these words, he had sent her back to her family, Camille pulled herself together.

'I've got nothing to say to them. I think those things are my business. I don't care for family councils.'

'I agree with you—for the moment.'

'In any case we can decide, from tomorrow…'

He raised his free hand, to fend off the threat for the future.

'No, not tomorrow. Today there's no tomorrow.'

As he was going out of the bedroom, he turned round.

'I've left my key and the money we have here in the bathroom.'

She interrupted him sarcastically:

'Why not a crate of tinned food and a compass?'

She was putting on a brave face, looking straight at him, one hand on hip, her head held erect on her beautiful neck.

'She's making a big thing of my exit,' Alain thought. He wanted to reply with a similar last-minute flourish, to throw back his hair from his forehead, to give her the narrow look between his eyelashes and stare her straight in the face; but he gave up trying as it was incompatible with holding the shopping basket, and he made do instead with a vague wave in Camille's direction.

She kept her countenance, theatrically. A little way off, before he left, he could see more clearly the dark circles round her eyes and the dampness on her forehead and flawless neck.

Downstairs he automatically crossed the street, with the garage key in his hand. 'I can't do that,' he thought, and retraced his steps towards the avenue, quite a long way off, where you could pick up a cruising night taxi. Saha meowed two or three times and he spoke soothingly to her. 'It would be a lot more convenient to take the car, but I can't do it. Neuilly's impossible at night.' He was surprised that, being now on his own, he was losing his confidence, because he had counted on a blessed sense of release, but walking didn't calm him. At last he came across a cruising taxi but found the five-minute drive long.

In the warm night under the gaslight he shivered as he waited for the gate to open. Saha, who recognized the smell of the garden, was mewing continually in the basket he'd put down on the pavement.

The scent of the wisteria in its second flowering pervaded the air, and Alain shook even more, shifting his weight from one foot to the other as though it were very cold. He rang again, for nothing was stirring in the house, despite the solemn, shocking reverberation of the great bell. At last a light appeared in the garage outbuildings and he could hear old Émile's feet dragging along the gravel.

'It's me, Émile,' he said when the old retainer's colourless face appeared at the grid.

'Monsieur Alain?' Émile said, quavering more than ever. 'Monsieur Alain's young lady's not poorly? Summer's so treacherous…I see that Monsieur Alain has a case with him?'

'No, that's Saha. Leave her, I'll carry her. No, don't light the garden lamps, they might wake Madame. Just open the main gate for me and go back to bed.'

'Madame is awake, she woke me up, I didn't hear the loud bell. I'd just fallen fast asleep, you see…'

Alain hurried in, to avoid the string of words and the sound of the unsteady footsteps following. He didn't stumble at the bends in the path, although the night was moonless. The vast lawn, paler than the cultivated flower beds, guided him. The shrouded dead tree in the middle of the lawn looked like a very tall man standing with his coat on his arm. The scent of the watered geraniums brought Alain up short and his throat tightened. He bent down, fumbling at the basket, opened it and set Saha free.

'Our garden, Saha…'

He felt her glide out of the basket and out of love for her, stopped fussing over her. He gave her back, dedicated to her, the night, her freedom, the spongy, soft earth, the waking insects and the sleeping birds.

Behind the blinds on the ground floor a lamp was waiting, and Alain grew sombre. 'Talk and more talk, explaining to my mother, explaining what? It's so simple...it's so difficult.'

All he wanted was silence, his room with the faded flowers on the wallpaper, his bed, and above all, the violent tears, great hoarse sobs like coughing, a secret and guilty compensation.

'Come in, darling, come in...'

He had not often visited his mother's bedroom. His selfish aversion to little bottles and droppers, boxes of digitalin and homeopathic medicine dated from his childhood and still remained. But he was powerless against the sight of the simple, narrow bed and the woman with copious white hair who was propping herself up on her wrists.

'You know, Maman, it's nothing special...'

This ridiculous sentence was accompanied by a smile he was ashamed of, a stiff smile, his lips not moving. His tiredness had suddenly undone him and was giving the lie to what he had just said, and he realized that. He sat down at his mother's bedside and untied his scarf.

'You must forgive the way I'm dressed. I came just as I was. I arrive at inappropriate times, without warning.'

'But you did give me warning,' said Madame Amparat.

She glanced at Alain's dusty shoes.

'Your shoes are like a tramp's.'

'I've only come from my house, Maman. But I was trying to get a taxi for quite a long time. I was carrying the cat.'

'Ah,' said Madame Amparat. 'You've brought back the cat?'

'Yes, of course. If you knew...'

He stopped, constrained by a strange discretion. "These are things one doesn't say. They are not things to tell your parents."

'Camille doesn't like Saha very much, Maman.'

'I know,' said Madame Amparat.

She forced a smile, nodded her frizzy head.

'That's very serious!'

'Yes, for Camille,' said Alain, malevolently.

He got up, walked around among the furniture, which was covered in sheets for the summer, as in provincial houses. Since he had resolved not to implicate Camille, he couldn't think what else to say.

'You know, Maman, there wasn't any shouting or smashed plates... The glass dressing table didn't suffer, and the neighbours didn't come up. Only I need a bit of solitude, a respite. I'm not hiding from you that I've had enough,' he said, sitting on the bed.

'No, you're not hiding that from me,' said Madame Amparat.

She put a hand on Alain's forehead, turning his young face with its pale stubble towards the light. Feeling sorry for himself, he averted his welling eyes and again managed to fend off the tumultuous rush of tears he anticipated.

'If there aren't any sheets on my old bed, Maman, I can wrap myself in whatever's to hand.'

'There are sheets on your bed,' said Madame Amparat.

When she said that, he hugged his mother, and, with his eyes shut, kissed her on her eyelids, cheeks and hair, nuzzled her neck, stammered out a goodnight and went out of the room, sniffing.

In the hall he pulled himself together and did not go upstairs immediately. The night which was coming to an end, and Saha, beckoned. But he did not go far. The flight of steps was enough. He sat in the shadow on a step and his outstretched hand encountered the fur, the subtle antennae of Saha's whiskers and cold nose.

She turned round and round on the spot, the demonstrative ritual of the wild cat. She seemed to him very small, light as a kitten, and because he was hungry, he thought she needed to eat something.

'We'll have something to eat tomorrow...In a little while...It'll soon be morning.'

She already smelled of mint, geranium, and box. He held her there, trusting and fragile, promised, perhaps, another ten years of life, and he felt sad when he thought of the brevity of their great love.

'After you, I shall probably be anyone's for the asking, a woman, women, but never another cat's.'

A blackbird whistled four notes which echoed across the whole garden and then was quiet. But the sparrows had heard him and answered. On the lawn and on the flower beds the ghosts of colours were appearing. Alain could make out a dull white, a deadened red, gloomier than black, a yellow one sticking out of its surrounding greenery, a round yellow flower that soon got yellower, succeeded by eyes and moons...Unsteady on his feet, engulfed by sleep, Alain reached his bedroom, threw off his clothes, turned back the bedclothes, and surrendered himself completely to the cool sheets.

Lying on his back with one arm stretched out, with the cat silent and intent, kneading his shoulder, he was descending headlong first into the deepest of sleeps, when he was brought back with a start to the first light of day, the swaying of the trees waking up and the blessed creaking of the tram in the distance.

'What's the matter with me? Oh, I know, I was wanting to weep.' He smiled and fell asleep again.

He slept feverishly, gorging on dreams. Two or three times he thought he was waking up and became aware of where he was, but every time he was disabused by the way the walls of his room looked, hostile and as if watching for a winged eye that fluttered.

'I'm asleep, I tell you, asleep.'

'I'm asleep,' he said again at the sound of the gravel crunching. 'I keep telling you, I'm asleep!' he shouted at two feet dragging themselves along outside the door. The feet drew away and in his dream the sleeper congratulated himself. But because of all these repeated solicitings, the dream had reached its fullness and Alain opened his eyes.

The sun, which he had last seen in May on his window ledge, had become an August sun and did not pass beyond the satiny trunk of the tulip tree opposite the house. 'Summer has grown old,' Alain said to himself. He got up, naked, looked for some clothes and found some pyjamas that were too short for him and tight in the sleeve, and a faded bathrobe which he put on with great pleasure. The window was inviting him over, but he knocked against the photograph of Camille, forgotten by the bed. He scrutinized the glossy little portrait, inaccurately lightened here, darkened there. 'It's a better likeness than I thought,' he decided. 'How is it I didn't notice? Four months ago, I was saying to myself: "Oh, she doesn't look like this at all—she's softer and more sensitive." But I was wrong.'

The constant breeze whispered lengthily through the trees like the murmur of a river. Dazzled by the light, and hunger gnawing at the pit of his stomach, Alain gave in: 'How nice it is to be convalescing!' To crown this illusion, a finger tapped on the door and in came the Basque maid with the moustache, carrying a tray.

'I could have had breakfast in the garden, Juliette!'

The ghost of a smile showed through the grey hairs.

'I thought…But If Monsieur Alain would like me to take the tray down?'

'No, I'm too hungry, leave it there. Saha'll come in through the window…'

He called the cat who suddenly appeared from her invisible retreat, as though brought into life by his summons. She leaped up on to the vertical trail of climbing plants and fell back—she had forgotten her broken claws.

'Wait, I'm coming!'

He brought her back in his arms and they both tucked in, she on milk and *biscottes*, he on bread and honey, and scalding hot coffee. A little rose decorated the handle of the honeypot in a corner of the tray.

'It's not from my mother,' he guessed. It was a poor specimen of a rose, a yellow rose taken from a low branch, that gave out a powerful perfume. 'It's a little offering from the Basque maid.'

Saha, beaming, seemed to have put on weight since the day before. The frill round her neck stuck out, the four silky stripes between her ears were very marked; her gaze, like that of a contented despot, was fixed on the garden.

'How simple it is, Saha, isn't it—for you at least!'

Old Émile came in next and picked up Alain's shoes.

'One of the laces is nearly worn out...Monsieur Alain hasn't got any others? Never mind, I'll put one of mine in,' he bleated pathetically.

'It must be my birthday.' Alain said to himself. This thought made him turn his thoughts immediately to the opposite, to the concerns of what was yesterday routine for him, getting ready, what time he was leaving for the Amparat offices, what time he would come back to lunch with Camille.

'But I haven't anything to put on!' he cried.

He was delighted to find his old friends, the somewhat rusty razor, the pink egg-shaped soap, his old toothbrush, in the bathroom, and fell upon them with delight, as though playing at being a shipwrecked sailor. But he had to go downstairs in pyjamas that were too short, since the Basque maid had taken away all his clothes.

'Come on Saha, Saha!'

She went down first, he followed clumsily, his feet unsteady in frayed raffia sandals. He offered his shoulder to the cloak of mild sunshine and half closed his eyes, unused to the dazzle of the green lawns, the warmer and warmer colours given off by a tightly packed bed of love-lies-bleeding with fleshy heads, a cluster of red salvias surrounded by heliotropes.

'Oh! the salvias are the same, the same ones!' Alain had only ever known this little heart-shaped flower bed to be red and edged with heliotropes, protected by a spindly old cherry tree that sometimes produced a few cherries in September.

'I can see six…seven…Seven green cherries!'

He was talking to the cat who, her eyes vacant and golden, affected by the overpowering smell of the heliotropes, half opened her mouth and exhibited the nauseous ecstasy of wild cats subjected to overpowering scents.

She sampled a blade of grass in order to recover, listened to voices, rubbed her nose against the hard sticks of the pruned privet. However, she didn't show any lack of restraint or gay abandon, but walked with dignity under the little silver halo that encircled her wherever she went.

'Thrown off the top of nine storeys,' Alain thought as he looked at her. 'Grabbed—or pushed…Perhaps she put up a struggle…Perhaps she escaped and was captured again and tipped out. Murdered.'

With such conjectures he tried to summon up a justified anger in himself and failed. 'If I loved Camille truly, deeply, how furious I'd be…' Around him his kingdom shone brightly, threatened like all kingdoms. 'My mother assures me that before twenty years are up nobody will be able to preserve a house or garden like this one. It's quite possible. I don't mind losing it. I just don't want to let other people…'

The ringing of the telephone in the house startled him. 'Come now. Am I scared? Camille is not so stupid as to phone me. Let's give her her due: I've never seen a woman use that device as discreetly as she does.'

But he couldn't prevent himself running as fast as he could, losing his sandals and stumbling over the round pebbles, calling:

'Maman! Who's that on the phone?'

The thick white bathrobe appeared on the steps, and Alain felt ashamed that he'd shouted.

'How I love your big white bathrobe, Maman, always the same, always the same…'

'Thank you for the compliment,' said Madame Amparat.

She allowed Alain to wait a moment before she answered.

'It was Monsieur Veuillet. It's half past nine. Have you forgotten your office routine?'

She combed her son's hair with her fingers, buttoned up the outgrown pyjamas.

'That's better! I hope you are not going to spend the rest of your days looking like a tramp?'

Alain was grateful for her tactful questions.

'Of course not, Maman. I'll see to all that shortly...'

Madame Amparat affectionately waved aside his ample, vague gesture: 'Where are you going to be this evening, darling?'

'Here!' he cried, and his eyes welled with tears.

'Goodness, what a child you are!' said Madame Amparat, and he repeated the word with the gravity of a boy scout.

'Perhaps I am, Maman. I'd just like to get it clear in my head what I ought to be doing, to leave my childhood behind....'

'How? Through divorce? That's a bumpy road to take.'

'But it would give me some breathing space,' he ventured with some asperity.

'Would a temporary separation, a rest, or a holiday give as good results?'

He raised indignant arms.

'But, Mother dear, you can't imagine...You are miles and miles away from imagining...'

He was about to tell her everything, explain about the murderous attack.

'Well, let me stay miles away! Those things are not my concern. Kindly have a little...reserve,' Madame Amparat said hastily, and Alain took advantage of her discreet misunderstanding.

'Now, Maman, there is still the annoying aspect, I mean the family perspective which is all mixed up with the commercial one. From the Malmert point of view my divorce would be inexcusable, even if Camille is partly responsible. A wife of three and a half months... I can hear them already...'

'Where do you get the commercial point of view from? You don't have a business in common, you and Camille? A couple's not the same as business partners.'

'I know that, Maman! But if events proceed as I suspect they will, it's a horrible period of formalities, interviews...A divorce is never as simple as people think.'

She heard her son out calmly, knowing that some causes may produce unforeseen results and that a man is obliged throughout his life to be reincarnated several times with no other assistance than that of chance, of bruises, of mistakes...

'It's never easy to let go of what we have wanted to attach to ourselves,' said Madame Amparat. 'The little Malmert's not as bad as all that. A little unpolished, a little lacking in manners perhaps...No, not so bad. At least that's my opinion, but I'm not forcing you to share it. We have time to think it over...'

'I've taken care of that,' Alain said, with a surly politeness. 'And although I'd rather keep a certain event to myself at the moment...'

His face suddenly lit up with a laugh, as though he were a child again. Standing on her back legs, Saha was fishing drowned ants out of a full watering can, scooping them out with her paw.

'Look at her, Maman! Isn't she a feline miracle?'

'Yes,' sighed Madame Amparat. 'She's your chimera.'

He was always surprised when his mother used an unusual word. He greeted this one with a kiss planted on a hand, old before its time, with large veins, marked with those brown moons that Juliette, the Basque maid, lugubriously called 'earth stains'. At the loud ringing of the bell at the gate he drew himself up.

'Make yourself scarce,' said Madame Amparat. 'We're right in the way of the tradesmen. Go and get dressed. Do you want the butcher's boy coming across you in that garb?'

But they both knew that the butcher's boy never rang at the visitors' entrance, and Madame Amparat was already turning her back and hurrying up the flight of steps, lifting her dressing gown with both hands as she went. Behind the clipped euonymus Alain saw the Basque maid in full flight, her black silk pinafore flapping behind her, and the shuffling slippers on the gravel path also betrayed the vanishing of old Émile. Alain stopped him in his tracks.

'Did you open up, at least?'

'Yes, Monsieur Alain, the young lady is behind her car.'

He raised his terrified eyes to heaven, hunched his shoulders as though he were in a hailstorm, and disappeared.

'Well, this is definitely a crisis. I wish I'd got dressed. Oh, look, she's wearing a new suit.'

Camille had seen him and came straight over, taking her time. In one of those moments of emotion that are almost ridiculous and are occasioned by dramatic events, he thought confusedly: 'Perhaps she's coming to lunch.'

Carefully and lightly made up, equipped with black eyelashes, parted lips, and dazzling white teeth, she nevertheless seemed to lose confidence when Alain went forward to meet her. For he approached her without leaving his protective atmosphere, stepping on his native grass with the sumptuous collusion of the trees overhead, and Camille observed him abjectly.

'Forgive me for looking like an adolescent schoolboy...We hadn't arranged to meet this morning?'

'No, I've brought you the large case with all your things.'

'You shouldn't have done!' he exclaimed. 'I would have had Émile bring it over today.'

'Huh, don't mention Émile. I wanted to give him your case, but that old idiot rushed off as though I had the plague. The case is on the ground near the gate.'

Blushing with humiliation, she bit the inside of her cheek. "That's a good start," Alain said to himself.

'I'm sorry. You know what Émile is like. Listen,' he decided, 'let's go into the euonymus ring, we shall be quieter there than in the house.'

He regretted his choice immediately, for the rotunda, a little clearing surrounded by a clipped euonymus hedge and furnished with wicker seats, had in the past hidden their clandestine kisses.

'Wait while I remove the twigs. We mustn't ruin your pretty suit, which I haven't seen before.'

'It's new,' said Camille, in a tone of profound sadness, as though she'd said: 'It's dead.'

She sat sideways, looking around her. Two arching lines of trees could be seen through the two opposing gaps in the verdant rotunda. Alain remembered something Camille had once confessed to him: 'You've no idea how overawed I used to be by your beautiful garden. I used to feel I was the little village girl come to play with the son of the gentry in their domain. And yet...' With one word she'd spoiled everything, the last word, *yet,* which made him aware of the prosperity of the Malmert laundry compared with the decline of the Amparat's business.

He noticed that Camille had not taken off her gloves. 'That's a precautionary measure which does her no favours. Without those gloves I might not have noticed her hands and the terrible thing they did. Oh, at last I'm a bit angry' he told himself, listening to his heart beating. 'It's taken me a while.'

'So,' said Camille, bleakly, 'what are you going to do? Perhaps you haven't thought about it yet?'

'I have,' Alain said.

'Oh!'

'Yes. I can't come back.'

'I understand that you can't today.'

'I don't want to come back.'

'Not at all? Never?'

He shrugged.

'What does "never" mean? I don't want to come back. Not now. I don't want to.'

She watched him closely, trying to work out the truth from the lies, the deliberate irritation from the authentic shock. He gave her back suspicion for suspicion. 'She looks smaller this morning. A bit like a pretty little shop girl. She's lost amongst all this greenery. We've already exchanged a lot of useless remarks...'

In the distance, through one of the arcades of trees, Camille spied the signs of the new buildings, another window, shutters freshly painted. She made a brave, indeed reckless, move:

'Supposing I hadn't said anything yesterday?' she suggested suddenly. 'What if you didn't know a thing about it?'

'Typical female idea,' he jeered. 'It does you credit.'

'Oh!' said Camille shaking her head, 'credit, credit...It wouldn't be the first time that the happiness of a couple depended on something inadmissible or unadmitted. But I think if I'd hidden it from you I'd only have made things worse for myself. I didn't feel you were...what shall I say?'

She searched for the word and copied him, clasping her hands together. 'She's wrong to make her hands so obvious,' Alain thought vindictively. 'Those murderous hands.'

'Well, you're hardly on my side at all,' Camille said. 'Are you?'

Impressed by this, he agreed inwardly that she was right. He said nothing and Camille insisted in a plaintive tone that he recognized all too well:

'Say something, you nasty man?'

'Oh, for heaven's sake,' he burst out, 'that's beside the point! What I'm interested in—as regards you—is to find out if you regret what you did, whether you can't stop thinking about it, if it makes you ill to think about it...Remorse, I mean, remorse! There's such a thing as remorse!'

He got up in anger, walked around the circle of lawn, wiping his forehead on his sleeve.

'Oh,' said Camille, with a contrite and concerned expression, 'of course I'm sorry...I would a thousand times rather not have done it. I must have been mad...'

'You're telling lies!' he cried, keeping his voice down. 'You're only sorry you didn't succeed! I just have to listen to you to see you, with your little hat set jauntily on your head, your gloves, your new suit, everything you put together to make yourself attractive for me...If your remorse was sincere, I'd be able to see it on your face, I would feel it!'

His cry was low but hoarse and he was not quite in control of the anger he had fostered. The worn material of his pyjamas split at the elbow and he pulled away almost all his sleeve and threw it on to a bush.

Camille at first only had eyes for his bare, gesticulating arm, strangely white against the dark euonymus hedge.

He placed his hands over his eyes and forced himself to moderate his words.

'A small innocent creature, blue as the loveliest dreams, a little soul...faithful, capable of dying gracefully if what she has chosen in her life is not there...You have held that in your hands above the void and you opened your hands...You are a monster...I don't want to live with a monster...'

He uncovered his damp eyes, moved closer to Camille, searching for the words that would defeat her. She was breathing rapidly, her attention travelled from his bare arm to the face that was just as white, bloodless.

'An animal!' she cried indignantly. 'You are sacrificing me for an animal! I'm your wife, for goodness' sake! You're abandoning me for an animal!'

'An animal? Yes, an animal.'

Apparently calming down, he hid behind a mysterious, knowing smile. 'I grant you that Saha is an animal...If she really is one, what is there superior to this animal, and how could I make Camille aware of that? She makes me laugh, this barefaced little criminal, so indignant, so virtuous, claiming to know what an animal is.' But Camille's voice broke into the scoffing in his head:

'*You're* the monster.'

'Sorry?'

'Yes, *you*! Unfortunately, I can't tell you exactly why. But I assure you I'm right. I wanted to do away with Saha. That wasn't kind of me.

But the first thing that comes into a woman's mind, especially if she's jealous, is to kill what's in her way or what makes her suffer. That's normal. What's rare, what's monstrous, is *you*, is…'

She was having difficulty getting across what she wanted to say, pointing simultaneously to the circumstantial signs on Alain which could only be interpreted as near-madness: the torn-off sleeve, the trembling, insulting mouth, the cheek drained of blood, the wild shock of unruly blond hair. He did not protest, scorned to defend himself at all, but seemed to be lost in an exploration from which there was no return.

'If I'd killed or tried to kill a woman out of jealousy, you'd probably forgive me. But I laid my hand on the cat, so that was the limit! And you want me not to treat you as a monster…'

'Have I said I want that?' he interrupted her condescendingly.

She raised her terrified eyes to him and made a gesture of impotence. Sombre and detached, he watched the young gloved hand with disgust every time it moved.

'Now for the foreseeable future, what are we going to do? What's to become of us, Alain?'

His patience fast running out, he was almost groaning and screaming at her: 'We separate, we shut up, we sleep, breathe, free of each other! I shall go away, a long way away, under this cherry tree for instance, under the wings of this black and white magpie, or into the rainbow colours of the garden spray…Or to my cold room under the protection of a small gold dollar, a handful of relics and a Chartreux cat…'

He controlled himself and calmly told a lie:

'Nothing for the moment. It's too soon to come to…a decision… We'll see later.'

This last effort to be reasonable and polite exhausted him. He immediately stumbled when he got up to accompany Camille, who, clutching at straws, accepted this vague attempt at reconciliation.

'That's right, yes, it's too early. A little later…Stay there, I don't expect you to come to the gate. With your sleeve like that, they'd think we'd been fighting. Listen, I may go and bathe at Ploumanach, at Patrick's brother and sister-in-law's place. Because the very thought of living with my family at the moment…

'Take the sports car,' Alain suggested.

She flushed, thanking him profusely.

'I'll return it, you know, as soon as I get back to Paris, you might need it, don't hesitate to ask for it. In any case I'll let you know when I leave and when I am back.'

'She's already organizing things, putting out feelers, building bridges, pulling things together, mending, picking up the threads again. It's horrifying. Is that what my mother thinks admirable about her? Perhaps it is. I don't feel any more able to understand her than to make things up with her. How well she copes with everything I find unbearable. Let her go now, let her go...'

She went, taking care not to offer him her hand. But under the trimmed green trees in the arcade she dared to brush her beautiful breasts against him, in vain. Alone then, he collapsed into a chair and next to him on the wicker table, miraculously the cat appeared.

A bend in the avenue, a break in the foliage allowed Camille to see the cat and Alain at a distance. She stopped abruptly, made a little start as though she was going to come back. But she hesitated only a moment and rapidly walked away. For though Saha, like a human, was watching Camille leave, Alain was sprawling in the chair, his upturned palm like a paw, skilfully playing with the first green, prickly conkers of August.

THE MASKED WOMAN

HE had been watching the swirling masks in front of him for quite some time, vaguely troubled by their assorted colours and the synchronicity of two bands playing too close to one another. His forehead felt tight under his hood. A nerve pain was starting at the back of his nose. But he was quietly savouring an agreeable restlessness which permitted him to be unaware of time passing. He'd been wandering through all the corridors in the Opéra, breathing in the silvery dust on the dance floor, acknowledging some bored-looking acquaintances, and had fastened around his neck the indifferent arms of a very fat girl disguised as a sylph, presumably as a joke. Embarrassed by his domino, stumbling like a man in skirts, this doctor in a cloak did not dare take off either his domino or his hood because of his schoolboy fib:

'I'm spending tomorrow night at Nogent,' he'd told his wife the day before. 'Someone has just rung me and I'm very much afraid my patient…That poor old lady, you know…Just think, I was excited as a child about going to this ball. It's stupid, isn't it, a man of my age who's never been to a ball at the Opéra?'

'Very, very stupid, darling! If I'd known, I might not have married you!'

She laughed and he admired her rosy complexion, her long, smooth face, tapering delicately like sugared almond.

'Don't you want to go to the green and purple ball? Even without me, if you'd like to, darling…'

She had winced and given one of those great shudders that, at the sight of a slug or a very dirty passer-by, made her hair, her dainty hands, and her bosom in her white dress shake in disgust.

'Oh, no thank you! Can't you just see me in a crowd, handed on from one person to another? You know I'm not prudish, but it makes my hair stand on end! I can't help it!'

Leaning on the balustrade of the gallery, above the grand staircase, he was thinking about this timorous creature while contemplating the naked back of a sultana, and the two enormous square hands, with black-painted nails, which were grasping it. They were protruding from the braided sleeves of a Venetian lord, kneading the white female skin like dough…Because his mind was on his wife, he started when he heard a little 'hem-hem', her familiar little cough, nearby. He turned and saw, sitting astride the balustrade, a long, mysterious figure in fancy dress, a Pierrot, to judge by the cloak with enormous sleeves, floppy pantaloons, a bandeau, and white powder plastered all over what little skin was visible through the mask with the lacy bib. The fluid material of the costume and bandeau with a dark purple and silver weave shone like the eels they fish for at night with iron hooks in boats with resin lamps. Astonished, he waited for another little 'hem-hem' but it never came. The Pierrot-Eel, seated, was nonchalantly dangling his heel and kicking against the marble balustrade, and all you could see were two satin slippers, and a black-gloved hand, bent on the hip. Through the two oblique slits in the eye mask, carefully concealed in a web of tulle, only a dull glow of an indeterminate colour could be seen.

He nearly called out:

'Irène!'

But he restrained himself when he remembered his fib. Never adept at play-acting, he also gave up trying to disguise his voice. The Pierrot scratched his thigh, in a coarse, unembarrassed gesture, and the anxious husband breathed again.

'Oh, it's not her.'

But the Pierrot produced a gold-plated box from his pocket, opened it and took out a stick of rouge, and the husband, uneasy, recognized an antique tobacco tin, with a mirror inside, his most recent birthday present to her. He put his left hand on the painful region of his heart in a gesture that was so sudden and unconsciously theatrical that the Pierrot-Eel noticed.

'Is this a declaration, Purple Domino?'

Half choking from the shock, the waiting, the bad dream, he did not answer, but for a while listened to the scarcely disguised voice of his wife. The Eel was looking at him, straddling the balustrade, her head on one side like a bird; she shrugged, jumped down, and moved away. This move liberated her uneasy husband, and, with the usual lively jealousy restored, he resumed his thinking, and got up in a leisurely way to follow his wife.

'She's here to see someone, or she's with someone. In less than an hour I'll know everything.'

A hundred cloaks, purple or green, guaranteed he wouldn't be either noticed or recognized. Irène walked in front of him, nonchalantly, and he was surprised to find that she was softly rolling her hips and dragging her feet a little, as though she were wearing Turkish slippers. A Turk in emerald and embroidered gold caught hold of her as she went by and her slim body folded into his arms, as if his grasp would cut her in two. Her husband ran forward a few steps and reached the couple just as Irène cried out in flattering tones:

'You great brute!'

She moved away, at the same languorous, calm pace, stopping continually, musing at the doors of the open boxes, but hardly ever turning around. She hesitated at the foot of a staircase, changed direction and came back to the entrance to the front stalls, inserted herself into a dense, noisy group with the subtle expertise and precise movement of a blade sliding into its case. Ten arms imprisoned her, an almost naked boxer pinned her against the edge of the dressing rooms on the ground floor and kept her there. She yielded under the weight of the naked man, threw her head back with a laugh, concealed by all the other laughs, and the man in the purple cloak saw her teeth gleaming through the lacy bib. Then she quickly slipped away and sat on the steps that led to the dance floor. Standing two paces behind, her husband was observing her. She readjusted her mask, her crumpled cloak, tightened the bandeau encircling her head. She seemed as unconcerned as though she had been alone and set off again after a few minutes rest. She went down, put her arms round the shoulders of a warrior who invited her wordlessly to dance, and then danced with him cheek to cheek.

'That's him,' the husband said to himself.

But she uttered not a word to the perspiring dancer covered with chain mail and after the dance proceeded calmly on her way. She went off to drink a glass of champagne at the buffet, followed by another glass, paid, and stood there curiously watching the beginnings of a brawl between two men, surrounded by screaming women. She also took a wicked delight in placing her little black devilish hands on the white bosom of a startled Dutch girl with golden hair who let out a shriek.

Finally, her apprehensive follower saw her brought up short, as though she had run into something, by a young man sitting exhausted on a bench, fanning himself with his mask. She bent down to the handsome, fresh, and brutal face, condescendingly caught hold of his chin, and planted a kiss on the mouth that was panting and half open.

But instead of hurling himself at them and tearing the two mouths apart, her husband disappeared into the crowd. He was dismayed, but he no longer feared, or expected, betrayal. Now he was sure that Irène did not know the dance-drunk youth she was kissing, nor the Herculean boxer, he was certain she wasn't waiting or looking for anybody, and that she would abandon, like a sucked grape, the lips she was holding between her own and wander on a moment later, pick up some other stranger, forget him, and, until she felt tired and went home, just enjoy the outrageous delight of being alone, free, true to her animal self, of being the unknown woman, for ever solitary, unashamed, her incurable solitude and deceitful innocence restored to her by a simple little mask and an enigmatic costume.

DAWN

THE clinical suddenness of the breakdown in their relationship left him stunned. Alone in that house where they had lived as a married couple for some twenty years, he'd not yet managed, after a week, to escape from his stupor and start to feel sorrow. It was funny to see him struggling with himself when familiar objects disappeared, and scolding his manservant, childishly: 'Well, those collars can't have just vanished! And don't tell me I've run out of shaving soap, there were two sticks there in the bathroom cabinet! You're not going to pretend there's no shaving soap left just because Madame has gone!'

Anxious because no one was there to give him orders, he forgot when it was time to eat, returned home for no reason, left the house to escape, dangling and half choking on the end of a string that the imperious hand of his wife no longer pulled. He called his friends to witness, the unfaithful or henpecked husbands, embarrassing them, offending their reserve. 'My dear chap, you won't believe this! One can't make head or tail of it, Aline has gone. She's left, so there we are! And not alone, as you may well imagine. She's left. I could say it many times over, but I can't say any more than that. Apparently, these things happen to husbands every day. What's to be done, I can't get over it. No, I just can't.'

His eyes widened, he spread out his arms and let them drop again. He didn't appear to be tragic or humiliated and his friends despised him a little: 'He's going downhill, oh yes, he's going downhill. At his age it's a real blow.' They talked about him as though he were old, secretly not displeased to run down this handsome, greying man who had never suffered any disappointments in his love life.

'His beautiful wife, Aline...He thought there was nothing unusual about her suddenly going blonde at the age of forty-five, the shade of an artificial flower, or that she had changed her dressmaker, her shoemaker. He didn't suspect...'

One day he took the train, because his manservant had asked for a week off: 'As there's not so much work now that Madame's not here, I thought...' And also because he continued to lose sleep, only drifting off just before dawn after remaining alert as a hunter, keeping his motionless watch in the dark, jaws clamped and ears twitching. He left one evening, deliberately avoiding the house in the country he had bought and furnished for Aline fifteen years before. He bought a ticket to a big town in the provinces where he remembered he had once 'spread the word' and banqueted at the expense of the *Extension Économique.**

'A nice hotel,' he told himself, 'a restaurant with traditional French food, that'll do for me. I don't want this affair to be the ruin of me, do I? So let's have a change of scene. Travel, good food…'

During the journey he examined his figure, still erect, in the mirror in the compartment, and the grey moustache that concealed the slackness of his mouth. 'Not bad, Not bad. No, by God, I won't let it break me! The little minx!' This moderate, old-fashioned word with which older people still indulgently refer to the imprudent young was all he used to curse his unfaithful wife.

At the hotel he asked for the same room as the year before: 'the rotunda, you know, with a nice view over the square'. He made his supper of cold meat and beer and went to bed when the night was nearly over. Because he was so tired he thought that his escape would be rewarded by falling asleep immediately. Lying on his back in the darkness he savoured the coolness of the sheets, which were not quite dry, and went over in his mind the forgotten shape of the large bay window through the two high shafts of bluish light between the half-open curtains. He even slipped abruptly into sleep for a few seconds and then inevitably woke, since, when he moved his legs back, he unconsciously made room for the woman who, now absent both day and night, faithfully returned when he fell asleep. He woke and bravely uttered the magic words: 'Come on now, soon it will be light, be a bit patient.' The two blue shafts turned pink and he heard the pleasant din on the square, and the rasping wooden pails hooped with iron and the clip-clop of the horses' large, patient hooves. 'Exactly like the noise of the stables in Fontainebleau by that villa we rented near the hotel. When it was getting light, we lay there listening…' He shivered, turned over, tried to get back to sleep. In any case, the sound of the horses and the buckets had stopped. Different, more subdued, noises came up through the open window. He identified the dull thud of pots of flowers being unloaded, plants being gently watered, and the soft sound of great armfuls of greenery thrown on to the ground.

'A flower market,' the insomniac said to himself. 'Oh, that's what it is. When we had that trip to Strasbourg, we discovered a charming flower market under our windows just as it was getting light and she said she had never seen cinerarias as blue as...' He sat up, the better to fight a despair which came upon him in regular waves, a new and quite fresh despair, unknown till then. Under the nearby bridge, oars slapped on the sleeping river and the flight of the first hissing swallows pierced the air: 'It's our early mornings on Lake Como now, the swallows flying over the gardener's truck laden with fruit and vegetables, the scent wafted up through our window at the Villa d'Este... Oh God, have pity!' He still had the strength to blush at the prayer he had begun, though his memories and the pain of being on his own kept him bent over on his bed like a man with chest problems. Twenty years...all the dawns of the last twenty years, poured on to the head of a companion asleep or lying awake at his side, their pale or dazzling ray of light, their bird's call, their pearls of rain, twenty years...

'I don't want it to destroy me, but twenty years is not nothing, dammit...And yet before her, there were other dawns. So, let me see, when I was a very young man...'

But the only things he managed to summon up were the dawns when he was a poor student, those grey mornings at law school, warmed by bluish milk or alcohol, the mornings of furnished rooms, narrow washbasins, and zinc buckets. He averted his thoughts, tried to muster to his aid his adolescence and the dawns of yesteryear, but when they came, they were dismal and depressing, imprisoned in a miserable period of his life, arising from a rickety iron bed, marked on the cheek by a stinging slap, shuffling along in shoes with spongy soles...Abandoned, he realized there was nowhere he could escape to, and that he would struggle in vain against the return of the light, that the cruel and familiar harmony of the first hour of the day would always sing one single name, would reopen one single wound, each time raw and new. So, he lay down again and quietly fell to sobbing.

As soon as the gate fell shut and the lantern was swinging ahead of us on the gardener's wrist beneath the shelter of the shapely yews which now and again let through the merest drip from the heavy rain, we sensed that a safe haven was at hand, and we joked to each other that the incident with the motor car, which had just brought us to a complete halt in the middle of the countryside, belonged to the category of *pannes bénies*.*

In fact it so happened that the owner of the château, Monsieur B., the regional councillor, who stood on the flight of steps to receive two drenched and unexpected women travellers, knew my husband slightly, and his wife—a former student at the Scola Cantorum*—remembered seeing me at Sunday concerts.

By the first log fire of the season there rose a hubbub of merry conversation. My friend Valentine and I were obliged to accept a snack of cold meats and a glass of champagne; our hosts had barely finished their evening meal.

After some vintage plum brandy and boiling hot coffee, we were almost like old friends. The electric light, rare in that part of the world, the scent of blond tobacco, fruit, the blazing wood smelling of resin—I savoured these homely delights as though they were gifts from an undiscovered island.

Monsieur B., square-set, greying only a little, with the charming smile and white teeth of a man from the south, occupied himself with my friend Valentine, while I chatted to Madame B....but observed her rather more.

She was blonde, slim, dressed as for an elegant dinner party rather than for receiving two stranded lady travellers, and her eyes were surprisingly clear, of such a pale blue, they lost even that faint colour when they lit on any brighter hue. They turned mauve, like her dress, green like the velvet armchair, or cloudy in the lamp's flame, with evanescent shimmers of red like the blue pupils of a Siamese cat.

I wondered if her whole face did not owe its absent expression, its vacant amiability, the smile that was at times like a sleepwalker's, to those overly clear eyes. A sleepwalker she might be, but she was at all times exceptionally attentive to our every possible need, trying to make the two or three hours that our driver would need to spend repairing the car with the help of Monsieur B.'s mechanic pass more quickly.

'We have a guest room you're welcome to use,' Madame B. was saying to me. 'Why not stay the night?'

And she had a sort of lost look in her eyes, that seemed to express nothing but endless loneliness and a dearth of thoughts.

'You'll be all right here, you know,' she went on. 'See how well my husband is getting on with your friend!'

She was laughing, but her wide, vacant eyes appeared not to be listening to what she was saying. Twice she had me repeat a sentence, each time giving an almost imperceptible shiver. Morphine? Opium? But no addict ever had such rosy gums, that quiet brow, that warm, gentle hand, nor that young, supple bosom in her low-cut bodice.

Could she be a silent victim of marital abuse? No. A tyrant, even a Machiavellian one, would never utter the word 'Simone' so tenderly, nor let his glance rest so admiringly upon his slave.

'Oh yes, Madame, they do exist,' Monsieur B. was at that moment asserting to my friend Valentine, 'they do exist, couples who live eight months of the year in the country, don't leave each other's side, and don't complain about their life! That's right, Simone, such couples do exist, don't they?'

'They do, thank the Lord!' Simone replied.

And her eyes, scarcely blue, held nothing but a tiny flicker of yellow, hardly there at all—the reflection of the lamp on the belly of the samovar. Then she rose and poured boiling tea laced with rum 'for the road'. It was ten o'clock. A young man came in, bareheaded, and before any introductions were made, handed a few opened letters to Monsieur B. who, apologizing to my friend Valentine, flicked rapidly through his mail.

'My husband's secretary,' explained Madame B., thinly slicing a lemon.

I simply remarked:

'He's a good-looking man.'

'Oh, do you think so?'

She raised her eyebrows, as though surprised, like a woman who meant: 'That's never struck me before.' And yet this slim young man, not in the least self-conscious, impressed me by his resolute expression, the way he closed his eyes, and his sudden uncompromising

stare, fierce, quickly concealed, and more disdainful than timid,
which became all the more striking when he opened them again. He
accepted a cup of tea and sat down by the fire near Madame B., thus
occupying the other seat on one of those dreadful but convenient,
S-shaped settees, that it was fashionable in the 1880s to call *causeuses.* *

There was a lapse in the conversation, and I thought our very kind
hosts must be finding me rather trying. I said quietly, to break the
silence:

'How cosy it is here! I'll remember this evening spent in your charming house, even though we don't know what it looks like from the
outside...We'll still be feeling the warmth from this fire, won't we,
Valentine, when we shut our eyes against the wind in a little while...'

'Then you'll have only yourselves to blame!' Madame B. exclaimed.
'If I were you, I wouldn't mind the wind at all. I love driving at night
with the drops streaking down in front of the headlamps, and the rain
on my cheeks like tears. Oh, I really love that!'

I looked at her in some astonishment. A delightful flame of life,
perhaps suppressed initially by her shyness, blazed forth from her
whole body. She relaxed and with the most delightful naïvety turned
into someone gay, well-informed, knowledgeable about local politics
and the ambitions of her husband, whom she imitated teasingly,
mocking him in the manner of very young girls. There was no lamp
on the mantelpiece and only the crackling flames in the hearth, away
from the central light, lent colour and shade to this young woman,
whose sudden liveliness made me think of gay canaries, wakeful in
their cages at the time of the lighting of the lamps. The dark back of
Monsieur B.'s secretary was leaning sideways on the S-shaped armrest, which separated him from Madame B. above the elbow. She
turned, while speaking, towards her husband and my friend sitting
a little way away, and, as I got up to put my empty cup down, I saw the
young man's concealed hand squeezing, in a persistent and perfectly
motionless grasp, Madame B.'s bare arm above her elbow. Neither
moved, you could see the young man's other hand held a cigarette
that he wasn't smoking, and Madame B.'s free hand waving a small
fan. Happy and attentive to everyone and clear-eyed, she was speaking in a voice occasionally interrupted by more rapid intakes of
breath, as though she was trying not to laugh, and on one of her hands
I noticed the veins were swelling, the secret squeeze was so tight and
passionate.

Like someone who feels the weight of others' eyes upon him, Monsieur B.'s secretary suddenly got up, said goodbye, and took his leave.

'Can I hear the sound of our engine?' I asked Madame B. a moment later.

She didn't answer. She was gazing at the fire, leaning her head slightly towards a sound she couldn't quite interpret and the sudden weakness in her body was like that of a woman who has just had a rather nasty fall. I repeated my question; she shivered:

'Yes, I think so,' she said quickly. She blinked, gave me a gracious smile which froze on her lips, her eyes filled once more with cold emptiness:

'What a pity!'

We left, carrying autumn roses and black dahlias. Monsieur B. walked alongside the motor car which was pulling away slowly, until we reached the first bend in the driveway. Madame B. stood on the lighted steps, smiling, her face drained of that fleeting certainty of being alive; one of her hands reached up under the gauzy scarf and squeezed her bare arm above the elbow.

HE had fallen asleep on his young wife's shoulder, and she was proudly supporting the head of this blond, healthy young man whose eyes were closed. He had slipped his sturdy arm under her light torso, under the adolescent hips, and his strong hand was resting flat on the sheet, next to the young woman's right elbow. She smiled when she saw the hand of a man lying there like an autonomous object, separated from its master. She allowed her eyes to wander around the half-lit room. Under a lampshade a conch shell poured its periwinkle light on to the bed.

'Too happy to sleep,' she thought.

Too excited as well, and frequently surprised at her new state, for exactly a fortnight now she has been leading the scandalous life of the young wife tasting the delights of life with a stranger she loves. To meet a handsome young blond widower, expert at tennis and rowing, and marry him a month later: this conjugal affair was not at all unlike being abducted. She still felt like that when she lay next to her husband, as she did tonight, keeping her eyes shut for a long time before opening them again to relish with some surprise the new blue curtains instead of the apricot-pink ones through which the dawn had filtered into her adolescent bedroom.

A shudder went through the sleeping body lying beside her and, with the charming authority of a creature lacking physical strength, she tightened the grip of her left arm around her husband's neck. He did not wake.

'How long his lashes are,' she thought to herself.

In secret also she admired his lips, heavy and graceful, a brick-red shade, and even his forehead, which was neither noble nor large, but completely unblemished.

Her husband's right hand beside her also gave a little tremor and she felt his right arm taking her whole weight under the small of her back.

'I'm heavy...I'd like to get up and put out this light. But he's sound asleep...'

Feebly the arm twisted again, to free itself, and she raised her back to make herself lighter.

'It's just like lying on top of an animal,' she thought.

She turned her head a little on the pillow, looked at the hand placed next to her.

'It's huge! Well of course, he's a whole head taller than me.'

The light, sliding under the edges of an umbel of bluish crystal, was striking that hand and making apparent the slightest elevations of the skin, exaggerating the powerful knots in the bones and the veins engorged by the compression of the arm. A few red hairs at the base of the fingers were all curving in the same direction, like corn in the wind, and the flat fingernails with their grooves showing beneath the buffed surface were shining with carmine varnish.

'I must tell him not to varnish his nails,' the young woman thought. 'Carmine nail-polish doesn't suit a hand that...a hand that's so...'

An electric shock went through that hand so that the young woman did not need to search for an adjective. The thumb stiffened, fearsomely long, like a spatula, and pressed closely against the index finger. Then the hand took on the aspect of a villainous ape.

'Oh!' the young woman uttered softly, as though at an impropriety.

The blaring of a passing motor car pierced the silence with a noise so shrill that it seemed like an illumination. The sleeper did not wake but the affronted hand lifted and clenched, crab-like, waiting and ready for combat. The lacerating sound faded and the hand, gradually relaxing, let its pincers fall again, turned into a limp animal, crooked, agitated by little tremors resembling death throes. The flat, cruel nail shone on the unnaturally long thumb. There was a slight distortion of the little finger which the young woman hadn't noticed before, and the sprawling hand revealed its fleshy palm, like a creature's red belly.

'And to think I kissed that hand! How dreadful! Had I never looked at it before?'

The hand, stirring in a bad dream, seemed to be responding to that shock, that disgust. It gathered strength, opened wide, showed its tendons, its nodes and its red hairs, as though armed for a fight. Then slowly closing again, it seized a fistful of sheet, grasped it in its bent fingers, and squeezed and squeezed with the methodical pleasure of a strangler...

'Oh!' the young woman cried.

The hand vanished and the huge arm, rapidly removed from its burden, turned into a protective belt, a comforting rampart against all the terrors of the night. But next morning when the breakfast tray arrived with foaming chocolate and toast, she could see that brownish-red hand again, with its monstrous thumb arched over the handle of a knife.

'Would you like this piece of bread, darling? I'll butter it for you.'

She shivered and felt her hairs at the top of her arm and down her back stand on end.

'Oh no, no.'

Then, hiding her fear, bravely regaining her self-control, and beginning her life of duplicity, resignation, shameful, subtle diplomacy, she bent over and planted a humble kiss on the monstrosity that was his hand.

HE had taken her away from another man, this tall, magnificent blond who resembled a greyhound on a leash. He had followed her everywhere, made romantic overtures, and carried her off. They didn't even know what had become of the other man and they never found out. The other man behaved impeccably, like the defeated lover that he was, and ceased to exist for them. The winner—let's call him Armand, and the woman, Elsie—hardly gave him a thought, for Elsie loved him and moreover he was only concerned to prove his love and innocence by organizing the prison that is *la vie à deux*.* She played her part in this, flattered, like every woman locked away supposedly for love. After a few weeks of hotels and travelling, they inevitably ended up in a villa by a lakeside, where they honestly believed they had arrived at the very home of happiness.

A certain lethargy, attending to her beauty and taking her time over everything, made the daylight hours pass quickly for Elsie. The night-time, given over to sleep or love, didn't seem to last long. Having both duly declared that, between lovers, silence was golden, they could be quiet together with impunity for the time being. They only ever went out together, came back, wandered in the woods, one leaning on the other or he in her wake, she trailing a ribbon, the end of a veil, the hem of a dress, like a broken leash.

Being nowhere near Paris, their solitude was guaranteed; the spectacle of their love was enough to put off their closest friends. You don't mind going to visit a man with a passion, or a woman who's in love, but being with a happy couple who make no secret of their happiness irritates and offends our taste for amusement in moderation and a healthy equilibrium.

So they lived together all alone, with the oblivious, obtuse bravura of lovers. On those days when at twilight, the sky overcast, the wind falling silent and the storm about to break, when the whole of nature was brewing up for a disaster, she wasn't averse to seeing this stranger with his broad shoulders, fierce eyebrows, and rapid gestures sitting opposite her. For a woman always retains, deep down, trust in the man who abducts her.

Armand himself did not give a thought to what had happened to Elsie before they met, since he held her close night and day, and was unaware of his beloved's past life. Elsie's past, as far as Armand was concerned, consisted of a poor man, deceived, immersed in dark oblivion. He did wonder occasionally, as though he felt it were his duty: 'But what about *before* that poor man?' and then returned to the present, unclouded by secrets.

The harm was done one morning while he was contemplating the lake and its pewter-rose mist behind a flaming hedge of crimson geraniums, when Elsie was upstairs singing a little tune to herself as she got dressed. It crossed his mind that he didn't know this song and that Elsie had never sung it before. He was shocked, and guessed that she was thinking about her past, about people whose names he didn't know, perhaps about a man he didn't know...

When his lover rejoined him, he thought she was a little different from the woman he was expecting and said so, with tender solicitude. She answered, unsuspecting, that the first autumn rains made her feel a little chilly and spoke longingly and with a winsome gesture of dismay of gas heating, big wood fires, fur coats. So he stopped looking at her and, lowering his eyes, began to count up the number of months they had just spent together, and he thought perhaps she wanted to leave him. The image that he formed of Elsie's not being there took him back to the time when he was living without her and he trembled, remembering that in those dim and distant days he'd been able to live another life. He raised his eyes to look at Elsie and his heart was not melting with love, but pounding and feeling tight because he was thinking:

'I'm just like other men, Elsie's just like other women, except she's prettier. The man I took her away from has probably become a man like other men, a man unburdened by happiness, a normal, sad, *lighter* man. The man who will take my place...'

He got confused, stopped his cogitations and realized that, bent low, he was entering into an unfounded jealousy, a jealousy that cannot be cured by guiltlessness.

He hid his feelings as well as he could, redoubling his demands on her love. But the care he took to repress his real thoughts made his head ache, and this rapidly had an effect on his sensitive lover. He struggled against it, his face and words convincing as ever, and it was Elsie whose health was affected, she gave nervous yawns and shivered when one night of the full moon she saw the shadow of Armand on the wall, standing there, expressive and alive, like a third person...He noted her malaise, put it down to regret, to her desire for escape, and one day roundly chastised her; she was reassured and flattered by this outburst. He grumbled to himself:

'Oh, it's like prison! A locked and bolted harem...'

But at the same time, he was doubtful about any cure, anxious when separated from her for even a few moments, yet not pleased when the woman he could not do without appeared again. These days he looked for flaws in her, and it grew worse when, longing for some peace from it, he found in her new signs of ageing, but hated her when she was not so attractive today as she was yesterday or the day after, and seemed to be assenting to his hostile will.

He lived in the state of distraction that is the punishment for those whom love has abused by making them believe in a new earthly paradise. He even tried to distance himself from Elsie with futile pretexts, but he returned each time more agitated and vindictive than before, for he was not away from her for long enough to get a foothold in the territory of more usual pain, the pain of privation, and the relief of having left his lover gave way immediately to the intolerable supposition that she had fled during his absence.

One day when he had left Elsie in the villa and was walking on his own by the lakeside, and subjecting his aberration to a sort of discipline without hope, he heard someone running after him, turned round and saw one of Elsie's maids, strange and distraught in her appearance, who halted, breathless, a few paces from him.

'Oh Monsieur...Madame...'

He shouted, in a high, unnatural voice:

'Madame, yes? She's just left, is that it?'

The maid opened and closed her mouth, could not speak straight away, then uttered a word or two from which the man understood that an accident...a fall on the marble steps...fractured her skull...instant death...death...He sat down in relief on the grassy bank:

'Oh!' he sighed, 'I was so afraid...'

THE man who takes his fox for a walk in the Bois de Boulogne is undoubtedly a decent fellow. He thinks it will please the little fox, who was perhaps his companion in the trenches, tamed during the terrible noise of the bombardments. The fox man, with his captive following like a little dog on the end of a chain, is unaware that out in the fresh air, the fox is only a lost soul filled with despair in an environment that perhaps recalls his native woods, an animal blinded by the forgotten light, drunk with scents, ready to run, attack or escape—but whose neck is imprisoned in a collar...Apart from all those things, the good little tame fox loves his master and follows him, his hindquarters and his beautiful tail the colour of lightly toasted bread trailing along the ground. He laughs easily—a fox is always laughing. He has lovely velvety eyes—like all foxes—and that's all I can say about him.

The other decent fellow, the hen man, always emerged from the Auteuil* metro at about half past eleven. He carried a dark fabric bag over his shoulder, rather like the tucker bag carried by tramps, and, walking smartly, reached the quiet of Auteuil wood. The first time I saw him, he'd placed his mysterious bag on a bench and was waiting for me to pass with my dogs. When I reassured him, he carefully shook his bag and there fell out, gleaming, the red coxcomb and feathers in autumnal colours of a cock and a hen who, without a moment's delay, started pecking around, scratching at the new moss and the earth on the forest floor. I didn't ask pointless questions, but the hen man briefly told me:

'I bring them out every lunchtime if I can. That's only fair, isn't it? Animals that live in apartments...'

By way of an answer, I complimented him on the cockerel's beauty and the liveliness of the hen. I added that I was also a friend of the little girl who takes her big tortoise out to play in the afternoons, and the man with the fox...

'I've never met him,' said the hen man.

But chance was to bring the masters of the fox and the hen together, on one of those paths you seek out when you feel like being on your own and want to avoid the wardens or indulge the fancy of a dog, a fox, or a hen. At first the fox man wasn't visible. Sitting in the undergrowth, he was holding the fox around the middle of his snake-like body in a protective manner and was pleased when he felt his body grow tense. The fox's nervous laugh revealed his sharp canines, a little yellowed by lack of exercise and soft food, and his white whiskers, which looked as if they had been groomed, flattened against his cheeks.

Some feet away the cockerel and the hen, gorged on seeds, were taking their bath of sand and sun. The cock was combing his wing feathers with his iron beak and the hen, swollen up in the shape of an egg with her claws not visible and her neck distended, was covering herself in yellow dust like pollen. A small dissonant cry uttered by the cock alerted her. She shook herself and came over to her mate to ask:

'What was that you said?'

She must have had a warning sign from him, for she didn't argue, but stepped over to join him as close to the bag as possible—the bag, their prison but not a trap.

Astonished at this behaviour, the hen man nevertheless reassured his animals with a 'Come on now my chickies!' with clucking sounds that they recognized.

A few days later the fox man, believing it a kindness, gave his little wild creature this pleasure of Tantalus,* but thought it would be more honest to reveal his presence and that of his fox.

'Oh, what a strange creature!' said the hen man.

'But so intelligent,' added the fox man. 'Yet not in the least malicious. You could give him your hen and he wouldn't know what to do with her.'

But the little fox was trembling, with an imperceptible, passionate quiver beneath his coat, while the cock and hen, reassured by the sound of friendly voices and in any case dull-witted, were pecking around and clucking away under the velvety eye of the fox.

The two animal-lovers made friends, as you do in the Bois, or at a bathing resort. You meet, you chat, you tell each other your favourite story, you pour two or three confidences that even your close friends don't know about into the stranger's ear, and then when you reach Tram 16 you go your separate ways, not having divulged the name of the street where you live or the number of the house.

A little fox, even one deprived of all dealings with hens, would not be able to be in their company without experiencing serious distress. This fox got thinner, talked aloud in his sleep in his own yapping language. And his master, watching the fine, feverish nose of the fox turn aside from his saucer of milk, saw dawning in him from the depths of a green thicket in Auteuil, a wicked idea, not very clear, but still nasty, taking shape. That day he was chatting in a very amicable way with his friend the hen man and distractedly paying out a little of the chain of the fox, who took one step—or whatever you call that gliding motion where the ends of his paws were not visible and not one blade of grass disturbed—towards the hen.

'Careful!' said the hen man.

'Oh,' said the fox man, 'he won't touch her.'

'I know,' said the hen man.

The fox said nothing. Pulled back on his leash, he sat down again like a good little animal and his bright eyes did not convey what was going on in his head.

The next day the two friends exchanged their opinions on angling.

'If it weren't so dear,' said the hen man, 'I should get a permit for the Upper Lake. But it's expensive. It makes the roach dearer than in Les Halles.'*

'But it's worth it,' the fox man enthused. 'You should have seen what a chap caught in the small lake the other morning! Twenty-eight roach and a bream wider than my hand.'

'You don't say!'

'And I don't wish to blow my own trumpet, but I'm not so ham-fisted either. If you saw me casting the line…I make a cunning flick of the wrist, like this…'

He got up, let go of the fox's chain, and made a magisterial gesture with his arm. Something frantic, the colour of rust sped through the grass in the direction of the yellow hen, but the hen man's leg shot out and thwarted his attack and the only sound the fox made was a little yap. The fox returned to his master's feet and lay down again.

'If he'd gone just a little bit further…' said the hen man.

'Well, blow me down!' said the fox man. 'You say you are sorry to the gentleman straight away, my son. Whatever's the matter with you?'

The hen man looked his friend straight in the eye and read in his face the wicked, albeit imprecise intention in his mind. He coughed, choking in sudden, violent rage and almost jumped on the fox man who was thinking at the same instant: 'I'll kill him, him and his farmyard...' They both made identical efforts to resume normal life, and, putting their heads down, determinedly put some distance between themselves for ever, like good, prudent citizens who have just come within a hair's breadth of murdering one another.

WHEN Madame de la Hournerie returned home, after half a day entirely devoted to the hairdresser and the milliner, she threw her brand-new hat down so that she could examine her new hairstyle. At the subtle promptings of Anthelme, who styled himself 'Fashionable Coiffeur', she had, at fifty, just abandoned her chignon, a hairdo that had been all the rage in 1910, with the lovely bouffant, flowing mahogany hair, the waves and curls that covered her forehead and ears. She went home with her hair still mahogany-red, but drawn back *à la chinoise*,* smoother, lacquered, fastened like a glossy shell on the back of her neck and pierced, like a heart, with a small sparkly hairpin.

In front of her mirror encircled with naked bulbs, she flinched a little at this dizzying expanse of forehead so rarely seen, normally more successfully hidden than was her bosom; at her hard bright eyes, skilfully made up, but which the light could now reach, thus depriving them of their mystery, like the sun on a forest stream after the tree-cutter has passed by. She picked up a hand mirror and, in its reflection, saw the large bun of glossy hair with its jewelled hairpin on the nape of her neck.

'Say what you like,' she said aloud to convince herself, 'it's very smart. Anyway, Émilie de Séry assured me just now that I was a real revelation.'

But face to face with this lady with the lacquered hair, the broad cheeks sagging slightly, the slack mouth, the more evident nose, she didn't recognize herself and did not feel very comfortable. With a painter's art, brightening the colour of a landscape suddenly flooded with light in the sunshine, she added rouge to her exposed ears, her temples and under the arch of the eyebrows, and powdered her whole face with a shade of pink she didn't often use.

'That's better,' she decided. 'Obviously it's a daring hairstyle! But why shouldn't I have a daring hairstyle, when all's said and done?'

She rang the bell and received ambiguous compliments from her maid—'All the changes Madame makes show her to her advantage!'—before she took off her day dress and went down to dine alone. In her elegant widowhood, which dated from five years ago, Madame de la Hournerie was not afraid of a few hours' solitude, and frequently dined or lunched on her own, as a pleasurable and hygienic mortification of the body, just as she might have eaten yogurt or gone to bed at five in the afternoon.

Marien was waiting for her in his uniform, arms by his side, in front of one of the dressers. He stood six feet tall, pride of the house of La Hournerie, a blond, good-looking boy with fair skin and wild black Breton eyes. Madame de la Hournerie and her husband had taken him away at the age of thirteen from the fifty cattle he had been tending in the fields. Appointed as kitchen-boy, Marien was provided with a striped waistcoat with sleeves and white apron and moved very rapidly up through the ranks. He conquered his fear of the telephone, demonstrated his taste in arranging flowers both in vases and at table, suppressed his peasant accent, and learned to pad about very softly. A sort of instinct for what was right and proper also guided him later, after exchanging the piped costume of a valet for the morning coat of a *maître d'hôtel*, only very discreetly increasing the amount when he ordered fruit, cut flowers, furniture wax, or metal polish. In return Madame de la Hournerie prematurely awarded him the supreme status of 'treasure' normally reserved for servants who were white-haired or enfeebled. But Marien, that muscular, silent statue, would never manage to extinguish the expressive fire of the severe black light in his eyes, gazed into by maids as though they were mirrors, luminaries that inflamed now a milliner, now a paper girl.

Madame de la Hournerie walked briskly into the dining room, sat down, and gave a little shiver.

'Please serve me at once, Marien. It's rather cold in here, isn't it?'

Marien, standing in front of the dresser, had not yet moved.

'I'm talking to you, my dear boy,' said Madame de la Hournerie in familiar tones; she still treated Marien simply like a 'young valet'.

'But the heating is at eighty,' came a hesitant voice.

Madame de la Hournerie, who was feeling the cold in two newly-exposed sensitive places—forehead and ears—looked up at Marien who, trying to hide his embarrassment, emptied his full ladle into the soup plate, served Madame de la Hournerie, and returned to his traditional place to stand facing his mistress. The *maître d'hôtel*'s dark eyes, wide as saucers, wearing an indefinable expression of horror and shame, were fixed on the vast bare forehead that resembled white marble and the skullcap of lacquered hair which matched the red mahogany Empire furniture. Uncomfortably Madame de la Hournerie pushed away her soup.

'Bring me the next course, Marien. I'm not very hungry. It wouldn't surprise me if I had a touch of influenza.'

Marien took away the soup, ran to the kitchen as though escaping, and brought in a shrimp soufflé. As he served it, he chipped the edge off an antique plate, spilled a few drops of red wine on the tablecloth, then went back to the sideboard and resumed his horrified contemplation.

'Influenza is going round,' Madame de la Hournerie went on, in some discomfort. 'Take care when you are in the kitchen. Henriette was complaining of aches and pains this morning. Take this soufflé away, the shrimps are dry. And you don't seem to be yourself either this evening...'

'It's the season,' came the same hesitant voice.

But the pitiless and truthful black eyes of Marien staring at her cried out to Madame de la Hournerie between each course 'No, it's not the *season*! It's the shock of your forehead, that great expanse of pallid white, that tiny skull, that heavy fruit: the head of an old woman, shorn of the growth I was accustomed to seeing mature! It's the indignation of a bit of a pilferer, a servant who looks after and exploits this household but is nonetheless attached to it. It's the stupor of a former valet who served a beautiful mistress, of a young cowherd faithful to a memory that dazzled him. She can't do that. She just can't!'

The *nègre en chemise*,* bathed in its thick vanilla cream, had no more success than the rack of lamb or artichoke hearts. Unable to bear it anymore, Madame de la Hournerie tried to counter the importunate and silent disapproval. A trace of red powder in the chasing on a fork, a lampshade singed at the edges would have provided her with the opportunity. But, paralysed with cowardice before she could utter the first reprimand, she left the table and ordered sharply:

'Send Henriette upstairs to me.' She ran to her dressing room and sat down in front of the triple mirror.

'Is that you Henriette? Telephone Anthelme, yes, the hairdresser, tomorrow morning as soon as he opens. I want an appointment before lunch, do you understand? Before lunch.'

BIRDSONG crept incongruously and effortlessly into the dream of night trains with revolving plates and red lights jolting Pierre Lasnier back and forth on badly aligned rails. The exquisite song struggled to be heard but prevailed against the whistling of the locomotives and woke the man lying on his back asleep, his half-open eyes unable to take in the image of a narrow branch against a dazzling sky where a little bird was singing. Shocked, Pierre Lasnier closed his eyes again and pressed them tight with his right arm, which felt damp and cold. A bird...his damp, cold arm...He sat up and looked at that arm, the muscly, brown arm of a tennis player, bare to the elbow below a rolled-up shirtsleeve. Above him the narrow branch from which the singing bird had just flown off was still swaying. His nostrils filled with the delightful scent of half-dried hay: Pierre Lasnier had just woken, not in his house in the Rue d'Aumale, but under a hedge in a field still covered with parallel lines like soft waves after the harvest.

He yawned and stretched, pulling back his arms as recommended by the Müller method,* unstuck his shirt soaked in the abundant early morning June dew from his back, combed his hair with his ten fingers, and smiled vaguely up at the clouds, still pink, in a sky the colour of pale blue milk. A fiery red shaft slanted through the hedge on a level with the ground, denouncing the risen sun.

'Oh, how beautiful!'

He touched his cheek pensively and shivered as he felt his five-day growth. No, four. Monday, Tuesday, Wednesday, Thursday, Friday. A five-day growth. For the last five days the body of a woman had lain, apparently broken in two, terrifyingly motionless on the carpet in his house in the Rue d'Aumale.

He stretched his legs. His grubby tennis shoes, dried out now after getting soaking wet and covered in cow dung, had got shabbier in the last four days and one of the rubber soles had split open. The flannel trousers of a very light grey, the white cotton socks, the cellular shirt, the whole sporty outfit had in four days grown to look like cast-offs strafed with dirty marks, striped with green streaks of vegetation. The waistcoat, rolled up like a sausage and tied with string, served as a pillow by night and contained a few hundred francs—the money Pierre Lasnier had on him at the time of the crime—plus a watch.

Tethered horses were rattling the chains on their hooves and neighing in the direction of an invisible farm. Swallows darted out from some inexhaustible hiding-place and covered the meadow with their network of long, shrill cries. The mooing of cows and a rich, melodious sound which must be the sound of a waterfall drifted over on the wind. A little cowherd in the distance was chanting like a muezzin as the bright day grew a shade yellower.

Pierre Lasnier, an urban dweller, allowed himself to be seduced by such indulgence.

'Ah, the countryside! This is the life!'

Then he checked himself and said: 'It *was* the life!' and realized everything he talked about was now in the past.

'I could just as well have spared that girl's life. But in Paris you live on your nerves. She was driving me crazy, she'd been annoying me for ages.'

He bowed his head at the thought of his insufferable mistress, his ears still ringing with all those threats, all that jealousy, words, reproach, with that insectile, fearless, unremitting nastiness that knew nothing of fear and rest. He again saw the movement that had turned his gesticulating hands into the hands of a criminal, the body doubled up on the carpet, and the time he had waited in the bachelor pad with the shutters closed; the escape at an opportune moment when the maid on the first floor rang to be let out and led a nice-looking boy in soft slippers across the road.

'I've been stupid,' thought Pierre Lasnier. 'I should have gone to the police station straight away and said "This is what I've done. She was such a nasty piece of work. We quarrelled thousands of times. I'm not guilty of premeditation, nor...well, I'm not wicked. I used to give her two thousand francs a month. And that day we'd come from the country just to pick up some tennis rackets in my flat." That's what I ought to have told them. They will have found her by now.'

In his mind he went over his four days as a tramp and no longer dared congratulate himself on not having met an officer patrolling the countryside. What did that prove? Four days was nothing. What happens after that? He made an effort to imagine some kind of future but saw only a whitish blur, the pallor making him feel physically sick.

'I'm dying of hunger! That's what's the matter with me. That's why I'm so depressed.'

He got up, grasped the stick he'd cut two days before that completed his tramp's costume. After supper the previous day—bread and sausage eaten as he went along—he was hungry as a hunter, being a healthy man. He jumped over the ditch, set off on the dusty road that was crying out for rain and cracking like shattered glass under his feet.

'And why did I eat bread and sausage on the way? What was stopping me going to a café and ordering meat, coffee, eggs?'

He shrugged and strode out. The thought of hot coffee and an omelette sizzling in the pan made his mouth water. But he walked cautiously past isolated farms, with brightly coloured hens, farmers' wives in white bonnets, past the red hearths where cauldrons hung on their pothooks. At nearly seven o'clock he passed through a large village and stopped at the last house where Cœuvre was offering 'Accommodation for walkers and horses and food for all'. As he was looking, a young woman with a braided chignon in the low-ceilinged room put down her child and wiped her hands. Pierre Lasnier sat down.

'A jug of wine? White or red?'

Pierre Lasnier tapped on the table in the traditional country manner he'd learned in the theatre.

'White! And have you got any bacon?'

'Bacon? Yes.'

'And eggs?'

'I haven't collected the eggs yet,' she said looking worried. 'And at that price…'

'Don't worry, I've plenty of money. Enough to pay for a good omelette!'

The young woman brought a china jug, a very small opaque, thick-ribbed glass, and studied Pierre Lasnier uncertainly. He was dirty but not uncouth, and his whole appearance lacked any secret aggressive intent, the impenetrable indifference that so frequently conceals a real vagabond.

'An omelette? How many eggs?'

Pierre Lasnier laughed.

'How many eggs? How should I know? Six or eight…Yes, a nice omelette with six or eight eggs!'

The young woman opened her eyes and mouth astonishingly wide, said nothing, took her child on her arm and left. Pierre Lasnier, to make the time pass quickly, filled and emptied his little rustic glass three times, pulled a packet of cigarettes out of his pocket, and struck a match. But for some reason he let the lighted match fall again, turned, and saw in the door frame behind the blue shoulders of two gendarmes the suspicious face, white with fear, of the young woman with the braided hair.

'A TABLE for two? This way please, Monsieur, Madame. There's one table left facing the seafront, if Madame and Monsieur would like to enjoy the view.'

Alice followed the *maître d'hôtel.*

'Oh yes, come on Marc, it'll be like having lunch in a boat on the waves.'

But her husband restrained her, slipping one arm under hers.

'This one's better.'

'Here, in the middle of all these people? I'd much rather...'

'Please, Alice.'

He squeezed her arm again so meaningfully that she turned:

'What's the matter?'

He said 'shh' under his breath, glared at her, and led her to a table in the middle.

'What's the matter, Marc?'

'I'll explain later, darling. Let me order lunch. Would you like shrimps? Or eggs in aspic?'

'I don't mind at all, as you know.'

They smiled at one another, taking up the precious time of a very busy *maître d'hôtel* who was nervously dancing attendance and breathing heavily down their necks.

'Shrimps,' Marc ordered. 'And afterwards eggs with bacon. And cold chicken with romaine lettuce, then cream cheese for dessert? The house speciality? Let's try that. Two excellent coffees. And please serve my chauffeur, we are leaving at two. Cider? I'm not sure...Some dry champagne.'

He sighed as if he'd just been carrying a ton weight, looked at the pale midday sea, the nearly white sky, then at his wife, thinking how pretty she was in her little *chapeau de Mercure** with the long veil hanging over her face.

'You look so nice, darling! And the blue of the sea makes your eyes look green you know. You've put on weight since we've been travelling. It's nice, it's really lovely, really lovely!'

She leaned proudly across the table, showing off her curves:

'Why did you stop me taking that seat over by the window?'

It didn't cross Marc Séguy's mind to lie.

'Because you were about to sit next to someone I know.'

'And whom I don't know?'

'My ex-wife.'

She was silent and her blue eyes widened.

'What's wrong, darling? It's bound to happen. It's not important.'

Alice found her tongue again and plied him with the inevitable questions in their logical order:

'Did she see you? Did she notice you'd seen her? Point her out to me?'

'Please don't turn around straight away. She's bound to be looking at us...Dark hair, no hat, she must be staying here. On her own, behind those children in red.'

'Yes. I see.'

Shielded behind large-brimmed sun hats, Alice was able to get a look at the woman who fifteen months ago was her husband's wife. Marc had said they were 'incompatible'. 'Oh yes, totally! We got a polite and practically amicable divorce, it was discreet and quick. And then I started to fall in love with you and you were happy to have me. What luck our happiness didn't involve any blame or hurt anyone!'

The woman in white, the light from the sea reflected in azure patches on her smooth, glossy hairdo, was smoking a cigarette with her eyes half closed. Alice turned back to her husband, helped herself to some shrimps and butter, and ate with composure. After a minute's silence:

'Why didn't you tell me she had blue eyes like me?'

'It never crossed my mind!'

He kissed the hand stretched out towards the basket of bread and she reddened with pleasure. If she had been a plump brunette, she might have seemed rather animal-like, but her changing blue eyes and wavy golden hair gave her the appearance of a delicate, sentimental blonde. She was a devoted and blindingly grateful wife. Without realizing it, she was unashamedly straightforward and her whole person bore the very obvious signs of intense happiness.

They ate and drank well, and each supposed the other had forgotten the woman in white. Yet Alice sometimes laughed rather too loud and Marc was careful not to slump in his chair, pulling back his shoulders and sitting upright. They waited for their coffee for quite a long time, in silence. An incandescent river, the long-drawn-out reflection of the high and invisible sun, moved slowly across the sea and shone with unbearable light.

'She's still there, by the way,' Alice whispered abruptly.

'Does it worry you? Shall we go and have coffee somewhere else?'

'No, not at all! She ought to be the one to worry! Anyway, she doesn't look as if she's enjoying herself all that much, if you could only see her.'

'No need. I know what she looks like in that mood.'

'Yes? Was she always like that?'

He blew smoke out of his nostrils and frowned:

'Moody? No. If I'm honest, she wasn't happy with me.'

'How could that be!'

'Darling, you are crazy, so lovely to me…You are a love…you love me. I'm so proud when I see that look in your eyes…yes, your eyes… She…I'm sure I wasn't able to make her happy. Well, there you are, I couldn't.'

'She's hard to please!'

Alice was fanning herself nervously and casting brief glances at the woman in white who was smoking, with her head resting against the back of the rattan chair, with her eyes shut in an attitude of satisfied repose.

Marc shrugged modestly.

'That's right,' he admitted. 'What do you expect? One must be sorry for people who are never satisfied. We are so happy…Aren't we, darling?'

She did not reply. She was looking covertly at her husband's face, glowing, regular, at his thick hair, interwoven here and there with silky white strands, at his short, manicured hands, and for the first time she was uncertain, and wondered:

'What else could she possibly want?'

And while Marc was paying the bill, asking about the chauffeur, the route, until they left she went on staring at the lady in white with a sort of envious curiosity—that unhappy, complicated, superior being…

THE previous week, when the President of the Council,* calling on
the practical experience and regional influence of the Deputy County
Commissioner, had offered Maurice Houssiaux the portfolio for
Tourism and Agriculture, he had not swelled with these feelings of
officious delight, like a little schoolboy. But now he was thrilled by the
Minister's spacious office, its antique desk and Aubusson tapestry.
A little green, flowerless garden grew up all over the high, arched
French windows. The hollow back of a bewigged marble bust was
reflected in the mirror, and there was just a touch of a new deference
in the usual friendly familiarity of his principal private secretary.

Houssiaux initialled his first mail with a flourish.

'Will that be all, Wattier?'

'All for today, Sir. You're free now.'

'Do you want a lift?'

'No thank you. I'll prepare your work for tomorrow. Oh, and there's
that damn corn circular as well...And have you given any thought to
your speech for the Hotel Industry?'

'Yes but...'

'I've been thinking about it too. You must make a good first impression. Don't worry, I've got all evening. It's very important that you
don't blow it in the first month. And by the way, there are those two
people from your part of the world who have been waiting for two
hours...'

'What people?'

'The shorthand typists. Do you want me to get rid of one, either
one? You've only got a single post to fill.'

'What are their names?'

'Here they are: Mademoiselle Valentin and Mademoiselle Lajarisse.
Both from Cransac.'

'Lajarisse, Lajarisse...there are three hundred Lajarisses in my
arrondissement, sixty in my *quartier*.* Which one is it?'

'Shall I send them away? Shall I tell them to come back later?'

Wattier danced excitedly from one foot to the other with the agility
of a hairdresser or acrobat which he had abruptly acquired at the
same time as his situation with Houssiaux. Houssiaux repeated the

name, which had a ring of the Midi about it, as he affectionately contemplated his rather sad green garden. His cheeks, those of a man who had once been a handsome blond youth, were getting blotchy. And he carried his little round paunch uplifted by a belt before him like a relic cushion.

'I'll see them,' he decided. 'They're from Cransac, the cradle of my election. No one else with them?'

'They've all gone. It's always the bosses who stay on.'

'I'll see them on my way out. If I spoke to them in here, they'd be telling me stories about Cransac for half an hour. One at a time, don't you think? I don't want to cause any trouble.'

Wattier, with an unkind little laugh, made himself scarce and Houssiaux, his outdoor coat on and his hat in his hand, went next door into an office whose unappealing ministerial poverty—old, plastered walls and yellow pine desks—did nothing to diminish his good humour.

'Mademoiselle, are you from Cransac? Do sit down.'

'Oh, Sir...'

The big girl was stammering nervously but looking at him with the boldness of a slave aware of her worth. A rare brunette, certainly, an amber brunette with a small imperious nose, and fearless beneath that timid exterior.

'Ah, what stars they are, these girls from my neck of the woods!' said Maurice Houssiaux to himself while he asked Mademoiselle Valentin a few casual questions.

'Yes, Monsieur le Ministre...Of course, Monsieur le Ministre. I started as an accountant at Vanavan's in the Rue Grande, on the corner, you know where I mean? But I can type anything and I'm good at shorthand. It was my father who hung the bunting across the Rue Grande when people heard about your election, Sir, two years ago, if Monsieur remembers?'

She spoke to him in the third person like a servant but fluttered her eyelids like a girl in love.

'She's putting all her cards on the table,' Houssiaux thought. 'She's right. She could have whatever she wants. And it wouldn't surprise her to get it. She's from Cransac. What an ornament she'd be in the office, at my right hand.'

'One of my secretaries will let you know, Mademoiselle.'

She raised her big eyes, tapered in the corners like a thoroughbred mare's.

'Might Monsieur le Ministre let me be hopeful?'

'I think we could!'

He put out his hand and wrung the stricken damsel's cold hand, watching with pleasure as she bumped into a seat on the way out and got the wrong door. He went back to his office, where a long mirror brought him face to face with his image, the image, alas, of a large, slightly tubby man, going grey. He was more than usually upset by this. 'Well, you can't have everything. You reach a certain age...Oh, I forgot Mademoiselle Lajarisse. Supposing I get Wattier to send her away?'

But a small shadow was already visible in the doorway, and Mademoiselle Lajarisse, a woman in her fifties, slightly shrunk and with the odd wrinkle, wearing black cotton gloves and a cloche hat, was standing there silently.

'You're from Cransac, Mademoiselle? That's certainly a recommendation! I love our Cransac and our people.'

'I've been in Paris for seventeen years. Cashier, shorthand typist, library work.'

'Good, good. We'll see, we'll see. No, no papers, you can give those to one of my secretaries, if necessary. Lajarisse? Which one? The one by the bridge?'

'No, the one on the hill up on the road to Casteix.'

'Ah, I see!'

He smiled and half shut his eyes. The hill up on the road to Casteix...He used to go down that road on horseback, greeted by everything in skirts, of questionable or seductive character: factory girls, women leaning leisurely over their balconies...

'I see...It's a long time ago!'

'Not as long as all that, Sir!'

Mademoiselle Lajarisse, from out of the past, looked him up and down from under her almost white hair.

'It was your favourite ride, Monsieur. Everyone back there remembers it.'

'I do too.'

He'd been a fine-looking boy, a flirt and a philanderer, untiring, enjoying all the adulation, women in all their moods, fast horses and fiery wines. Houssiaux could hear the flints flying on that steep hill under the hooves of his saddled horse. He nodded, half sincerely:

'Ah, Mademoiselle Lajarisse, how I wish I could be back in those days when I rode down the hill on my horse...'

'On your horse Gamin, Monsieur le Ministre…'

He made a delighted gesture, like a young man.

'Oh yes!'

'And on summer days you would arrive without a jacket or waist-coat, wearing a soft shirt, and your sleeves rolled up…'

'Oh yes!'

'You held the reins with one hand, you took off your hat and made sweeping bows to all the ladies…and even to the ones who weren't ladies…to that Carmen on her balcony, to the girl from the tobacco-nist's, to everyone…'

Houssiaux took the cotton-gloved hands into his own:

'Yes, yes! Do you remember all that?'

'Ah, Monsieur Maurice…!'

The little ageing lady looked straight at him and did not hide the two tears, or her blue eyes still shining with the indelible image of 'Monsieur Maurice' in the saddle. Houssiaux sighed regretfully and let go of the hands of Mademoiselle Lajarisse, who moved away a fraction.

'So, Monsieur le Ministre, do you think all the vacancies have been filled?'

He passed his fingers through his grey hair as he was wont to do back then when he was blond.

'Not yours, Mademoiselle Lajarisse. Have you got a minute? Here, take this shorthand pad. The pencils are there. Are you ready? "Dear friend and colleague, you have kindly drawn my attention to the fact that…"'

It was so easy to break into the little villa that the burglar, who had restrained himself so far through excess of caution, wondered why he'd waited so long. As soon as he went into the hall, he recognized that depressing smell of damp that pervades seaside houses in rainy summers. From the hall he found the door of the sitting room open, the dining-room door too and the one to the cellar under the stairs wide open, evidence of the haste with which the little red-haired maid, whose departure he'd been waiting for, had taken herself off to some dance hall or hollow in a sand dune. Madame Cassart had only one maidservant, knee high to a grasshopper: presumably she didn't need any more in her tiny villa with the pink plaster and the green mosaics, built on a sandy area, where the wind from the sea bent all the spindly tamarisks over in the same direction, like hairy grasses moving with the current.

The burglar carefully shut the rooms that were open; he didn't care for doors slamming and was hoping for a speedy visit to this ugly dolls' house rented by Madame Cassart for the season. A quick glance round the living room—white gloss and toile de Jouy*—no, the woman renting the house wouldn't think of hiding her savings in here.

The man walked around unhindered by the lack of light, aided by the pale night, a twilight grey, which stole through the closed shutters. Once he risked a flash of his electric pocket torch, which shone on to the photograph of a very beautiful woman in a long, corseted dress, her hair coiled in a figure of eight on her head and wearing gloves for a ball.

'The Cassart woman in her prime. She's changed.'

For the last two weeks in this fishing port, which had become ambitious and had suddenly been endowed with a fibro-cement casino, he had been leading the austere life of an entomologist, studying the customs and habits of bathers, especially female ones, making a note of the times they went out, what time they went to the funfair or dances each day. He'd had no windfalls since he arrived other than a gold purse, an unremarkable ring left in a washroom, and a reticule containing a hundred francs, meagre rewards in his scrupulous existence in which he strove to be totally transparent. He went to the casino, dressed correctly, trying to attract as little notice as possible, and didn't attempt to get to know anyone, for, although he knew he was a personable man in his forties with a thick head of hair, he knew the weaknesses of his syntax and the colourful brevity of his vocabulary.

'Just enough', he thought, 'to impress the girls in the sweetshop—and the Cassart woman.'

He'd been spying on her for two weeks, on the 'old madwoman' as everybody called her, this tall lady in her seventies who still had the figure of a girl in her old-fashioned clothes, a straight back in her tight corset, and the shoulders of a Prussian officer. Her organdie hats, her dresses of broderie anglaise, and her long rose-pink or orchid-purple veils flapped like bunting on the jetty, and the schoolboys behind her would overtake her so they could see her face; she looked like death warmed up, with waxy lumps on her cheeks and a neck squeezed tight by whalebone tulle above them.

He had marked her out at the famous sweet-shop, her jewels jangling, and pink as a wrinkled wax fruit; he'd waited while she greedily carried away a bag of chocolate pralines. When she had drifted off, scandalous and serene, he bought a box of sugared almonds.

'Shall I send them to the Hotel Beauséjour? For Monsieur...?'

'Monsieur Paul Dagueret.'

'With a D apostrophe?'

He directed a careless smile at the blonde shopgirl.

'As you please, Mademoiselle. It's of no importance.'

Rather taken with this aristocratic insouciance, the blonde shopgirl allowed herself to make a joke or two about Madame Cassart, deploring the fact that diamonds like that...

'I didn't notice,' interrupted Monsieur Dagueret, coldly. 'I'm not a connoisseur of these things.'

At present in the Cassart woman's room he was not looking for the diamonds she always wore, but for his just reward, owed to him because of his tireless, solitary effort:

'Even if it was just a gold necklace, or those thick bangles she puts on her podgy arms,' he muttered, poking about silently in the light, characterless room on which Madame Cassart had stamped her own taste by pinning bows and coloured beige flowers on everything.

As he flashed his torch in a drawer to see what was in it, he passed over an aquamarine cross, but picked up a gold propelling pencil worth at least fifty francs. At that precise moment he heard the musical creak of the garden gate, and then the sound of a key in the lock below. Someone was already labouring upstairs when he decided to take refuge behind the unfastened curtains at the French windows.

He immediately felt cross and uneasy. As a rule, the old madwoman never came back from the casino before midnight. Through the gap in the curtains he could see her walking back and forth grumbling to herself. She no longer took the trouble to throw back her military shoulders, she was bent, and she *munched*, in the manner of the elderly. She removed her girlish hat with care, took out her hairpins, and the prisoner could see a little white tonsure surrounded by a mass of hair dyed fierce red. The low-cut dress was cast off, a beribboned housecoat hid the grainy skin, spotted red by the salty air, and the ghastly rolls of fat on her neck. Under the flowing hair the angry face, made up as though for a play, increased Monsieur Paul Dagueret's discomfort.

'What shall I do?' he wondered. 'Obviously I'll do what I have to, but…an old cow like that, it's not nothing! Oh dear…!'

He did not like noise or blood, and every second added to his problems. Madame Cassart spared him any further anxiety. She turned her head abruptly towards the curtains as though she had suddenly caught his scent, opened them, and uttered a cry hardly louder than a sigh and took three paces back, hiding her face in her hands. He was about to take advantage of this unexpected gesture to make a run for it, when, with her hands still over her face, she addressed him in an emotional, pleading voice:

'Why did you do that? Why?'

He was standing between the drawn curtains, hatless—you invariably lose your hat or your cap—with his gloves on and his hair dishevelled. She went on, in the clear shrill voice of certain old people:

'You shouldn't ever have done that!'

She spread her hands and he saw, with stupefaction, that she was looking fearlessly at him, in a way that was both submissive and amorous.

'That's it. Now's the moment,' he thought.

'Did you need to be so violent?' sighed Madame Cassart. 'The most mundane approach at the casino or on the jetty, would that not have been enough? Can you believe I didn't notice or guess anything? It was very easy for you to…But not like this! not like this!'

She pulled herself up, pushed her hair back on top of her head, and wrapped her clothes around her like a dignified old clown.

The man, embarrassed, said nothing, then responded automatically, after a silence:

'If you'd ever...'

She interrupted him, trembling:

'No, no, don't say anything, you'll never know how upset I am...I am...My reputation is unsullied...I've never married... People call me Madame but...your being here...Oh, can't you see how upset I am...You won't get far with me like this, I swear!'

Each of her gestures and sighs made her diamonds flash aggressively, but the burglar, a sane and in any case shy man, paid no attention, but was only irritated. He nearly burst, and almost told this enraged old woman—and in no uncertain terms—what he thought of her. He stepped forward and saw his own face reflected in a mirror, the flattering reflection of a handsome and, my word, such a distinguished young man, dressed in black.

'Tell me I shall see you again, but not in my house for now,' simpered the madwoman. 'Give me your word as a gentleman!'

...Distinguished, perhaps, so long as he didn't open his mouth. A sort of snobbery removed all his wish to insult her, to hurt her, a snobbery which respected the outrageous error the old woman had made, and this moment in his own life, which resembled that of a noble and romantic hero. He bowed to the best of his ability and said in a deep voice:

'You have my word of honour, Madame!'

And he left, empty-handed.

OLD Monsieur Mestre emptied another watering can on to the bleed-
ing hearts, another on the heliotropes he'd just planted, and two on
the blue hydrangeas which were always dying of thirst. He tied back
some nasturtiums which had crept so vigorously over everything, cut
off the last of the dead cones of lilac with a pair of scissors, cried 'Ha!',
and rubbed his hands covered in earth. His little garden in Auteuil,
manured, watered, arranged like a living room that was too small,
overflowed with flowers and defied the June drought. Up until
November it was a sight to behold, at least for people going past. For
Monsieur Mestre, bending for hours over his rectangular plot surrounded by walls, tended it from morning to night with the determination of a market gardener. He planted, grafted, pruned; he tracked
down the slugs, the small suspicious spiders, the green aphids, the
leaf-curl insects. In the evening he clapped his hands together, cried
'Ha!', and instead of standing dreaming in front of the phlox, much
visited by the ash sphinx moth, under the white wisteria closely
entwined with the mauve wisteria, spurning the flaming red geraniums, he turned his back on his lovely work of art and went back
inside to have a smoke in the dining room, or took a little walk along
the boulevards in Auteuil.

The beautiful May evening had extended by an hour, after dinner,
this garden-lover's day. The sky, the pale gravel paths, the white
flowers, the white façades were hanging on to a light reluctant to fade,
and the mothers on the doorsteps of the little open houses called in
vain to their children, who preferred the warm dusty pavement to
their cool beds.

'Wife,' called Monsieur Mestre, 'I'm going out for a minute.'

Their house, typical of elderly houseowners of modest income, still
showed its faded bricks beneath the Virginia creeper. Around it, villas
of rich people had sprung up, *chalets normands*,* Louis XVI 'follies',
modern cubes plastered with vermilion red or cerulean blue.

Old Monsieur Mestre knew everything there was to know about
the fronts of the houses, all the rare trees in every garden. His curiosity stopped there; he wasn't envious of the little bells or the large bay
windows, big as fish tanks. While ensuring he didn't get to know too

much, he enjoyed speculating about them. He called a certain cottage with windows obscured by its covering of red trumpet vines 'Guilty Love', a certain little tower the colour of dried blood the 'Japanese Torture'. A regular white building with yellow silk curtains he called 'Happy Family', and Monsieur Mestre, gazing with ironic delight at a sort of pink and blue sugar lump in cement, marble, and sandalwood, had named it 'First Adventure'.

A 'native of the sixteenth *arrondissement*', he cherished the strange avenues like village streets, where a trusty ancient tree protects new houses that might disintegrate in a storm. He walked, stopped, patted a little girl on the head, clicked his tongue to scold a wailing infant. His hair, his silver beard provided a reassuring presence for the girls coming home late and they slackened their pace in order to stay under the protection of 'that nice old gentleman'.

The red and gold sky lasted for a long time on that starless May evening. But lamps were lighting up below and valiant nightingales were singing above the green benches and the rockwork pavilions. Monsieur Mestre looked benignly at a wide bungalow that he called the 'Broody Hen', spread out at ease over the garden. One single window with pink curtains was lit. At the same moment, a young man, hatless as is the fashion today, emerged from the house, slammed the door behind him in a rage, then the gate, and stood stock-still on the avenue, mulishly frowning as he gazed at the lighted window with a black, tragic look. Monsieur Mestre smiled and gave a little shrug.

'Another drama! And you can see straight away what's happened! We're eighteen or nineteen. We want to get our teeth into life. We want to be boss. We've had a scene with Papa and Maman and walked out, after saying some nasty things we very much regret…And we'd really like to go back. But our pride won't let us. Ah, these young things!'

Getting in the mood, he said in a quiet, fatherly voice:

'Ah! These young things!'

The young man swung round and stared coldly at the elderly silver-haired man who looked upon him with the gracious majesty of a soothsayer, gesturing at the lighted house:

'It's not here you should be, young man, it's in there.'

The young man gave a little shudder and stepped back.

'Oh no…' he said, dully.

'Oh yes,' Monsieur Mestre affirmed. 'Are you going to deny you were just going to go back in?'

The large black eyes, the still hairless lips opened in astonishment: 'How...how do you know that?'

Monsieur Mestre brought a prophetic hand down on the young man's shoulder:

'Hush! I know many things. I know...that you were wrong to resist the urge that was making you retrace your steps!'

'Monsieur...' the pale young man pleaded, 'Monsieur, I don't want to, I don't want to now...'

'Yes,' the indulgent Monsieur Mestre said teasingly. 'The great revolt, the escape, the bid for freedom...'

'Yes, oh yes,' the adolescent sighed. 'You know what it's like... revolt, escape...mustn't I...can't I...?'

Monsieur Mestre's hand came down firmly on his shoulder.

'No, no I say! Escape, freedom...they are only words! Unhappy child that you are, when you are a hundred paces away, you will be seized again by that strong urge which made you stop here, by that voice calling to you: "Go back! I am the truth, the kindness, the secret of that freedom you are searching for, I am the rest, the safety..."'

The young man interrupted the fine phrases of Monsieur Mestre with a look of inexpressible hope, flashed him a crazed smile and rushed back into the house.

'Bravo!' muttered Monsieur Mestre, congratulating himself.

After the slamming of a door he heard a young voice shout, briefly, as though muffled by a kiss. He nodded a blessing and moved away, happy, discreet, when the door opened again and the young man, panting, threw himself into his arms. He looked drunk, but was pale and greenish in the evening light, and he seemed a thing of wonder to Monsieur Mestre; his eyes full of unshed tears shifted from the sunset to Monsieur Mestre, to the cedar lit up with nightingales.

'Thanks to you...thanks to you,' he stammered.

'I don't deserve that, my boy.'

'Oh yes you do,' interrupted the young man, grasping his hands. 'I've done it. Thanks to you! For days and days, I didn't dare. I've put up with it all because I was so dependent on her. I knew she was being unfaithful and that every night...But I didn't dare! And then by a miracle I met you! You set me back on the right track again, you made me realize that running away wouldn't do any good, that I would carry away this torture with me...You showed me that deliverance, peace...oh peace at last!...depended on a gesture...thank you, thank you. I made that gesture, thanks to you.'

He let go of Monsieur Mestre's hands, started to run as if he had wings, soundlessly, his black hair sleeked back from his pale face. Then Monsieur Mestre felt his heart sink; he drew out his handkerchief to mop his brow and saw the red, bloody marks on it from the grasp of those damp, feverish hands.

WHEN he had killed her with one blow from the small lead weight, under which she kept her wrapping paper, Louis found himself in trouble. She was lying behind the counter, one leg bent across her, her head twisted and her body facing up, in a ridiculous posture which put the young man in a bad mood. He shrugged and almost said to her: 'For goodness' sake get up, you look a real sight.' But at that moment the doorbell rang and Louis saw a little girl come in and ask:

'A card of black mending wool please.'

He answered politely:

'There's none left, we won't have any till tomorrow.'

She went out, closed the door carefully and he realized that he'd not even thought she might have come to the counter, leaned over and seen…

Night was coming on, the little haberdashery and stationer's shop grew dark. You could still see the rows of white cardboard boxes with a corozo button or a ball of trimming on the side. Louis automatically struck a match on the sole of his shoe to light the gas jet, then remembered and stamped it out with his foot. The ground floor of the wine merchant opposite suddenly lit up and in contrast the little haberdasher's was plunged in darkness, with a stripe of yellow light.

Louis leaned over the counter again. With infinite astonishment he ascertained that his girlfriend was still there, leg bent and neck twisted. Apart from that, something black—it looked like a thin lock of hair—was trickling down her ashen face. He picked up the forty-five francs and the grubby notes he'd so furiously disparaged a short time before, went out, took the handle off the door, put it in his pocket and left.

Two days passed in a sort of childish trance, as he amused himself watching the boats on the Seine and the schoolchildren in the squares. Like a child he amused himself, and like a child he was bored. He waited but could not make up his mind whether to leave town or to establish himself up in the junk room as he had before. His room, rented by the week, still contained a stock of postcards of Paris monuments, mechanical jumping rabbits, and products in tubes to make a fruit drink. But Louis didn't open his shop for two days and slept in another furnished lodging. He did not feel afraid, he slept well; the day slid by, filled only with that feeling of pleasant anticipation you get in big ports when you have already got your ticket for the steamer.

Two days after the crime he bought a paper, as he usually did, and read: 'Shop assistant murdered in the Rue X...' He said aloud: 'Aha!' with the air of a connoisseur, slowly and attentively read the news item, noted that the crime, on account of the 'very quiet' life of the victim, was already being called 'mysterious', and he folded up the newspaper. In front of him, his white coffee was getting cold. The barman was whistling as he polished the counter, an old couple near him were dunking their croissants in hot milk. For a good while Louis remained in a stupor, his mouth half open, and sat wondering why these familiar things had suddenly ceased to be close and intelligible to him. He had the impression that if questioned, the elderly couple would reply in a foreign tongue, and that, as the barman whistled, he would be able to see through Louis's body without noticing he was there.

He got up, threw down some coins, and set off for a station where he took a ticket for somewhere in the suburbs, whose name reminded him of the races and of afternoons canoeing on the river. During the journey it seemed to him the train was making very little noise and that the travellers were speaking in subdued tones.

'Perhaps I'm going deaf?'

When he got off the train, Louis bought an evening paper, again read the same item as the one in the morning paper, and yawned:

'My God, same old thing!'

He ate in a little restaurant near the station and enquired from the manager about the possibilities of finding a job in the vicinity. But he went through this formality with great repugnance and felt uneasy when the restaurant owner advised him to go to a dentist's, who in a neighbouring villa was complaining about the departure of a young man who'd had a job the day before cleaning his motorcycle and sterilizing his surgical instruments. In spite of the lateness of the hour, he rang the dentist's bell, pretended he was a mechanical-toy maker, did not argue about the pay—one hundred and fifty francs—and slept that very night in a little loft room, with grey and blue flowered wallpaper of the kind they use to line the inside of cheap travelling trunks.

For a whole week he had a job as laboratory assistant to the American dentist, a great brawny red-haired man, who asked no questions but smoked with his feet on the table waiting for the occasional client. Kitted out in a white cloth smock, Louis took the air, leaning on the open gate, and the maids from the villas smiled when they saw his brown, gentle face.

He bought a newspaper every day. Banished from the front page, the 'crime of the Rue X' was languishing now on the second, in between the train crashes and the fraudulent activities of somnambulists. Five lines, ten lines, dispassionately affirmed 'it was a complete mystery'.

One scented, showery spring afternoon pierced with the cries of swallows, Louis asked the American dentist for a little money to 'buy some underwear', quit his white smock, and set out for Paris again. And as he was only an ignorant little murderer, he went to the haberdasher's shop straight away. Children were playing outside the closed iron shutters and the door, caked with mud from the week's splashes. Louis paced up and down for a long time on the pavement opposite and only left the street when night had fallen.

The next day he returned, a bit later so as not to draw attention to himself, and on other evenings he faithfully went back to his post after dinner, sometimes skipping his evening meal. He felt full of a strange anticipation akin to the anguish of being in love. One evening when he had stopped to look up at the stars and let out a long sigh, a hand was gently placed upon his shoulder. He closed his eyes, did not turn around, but fell limply, relieved, into the arms of the detective who was trailing him.

In the course of the interrogation, Louis admitted that of course he was sorry for his crime, but the moment when he had felt the liberating hand on his shoulder 'made up for everything', and he could only compare it to the moment when he had, as he said, 'fallen in love'.

THEY opened the two windows of their communicating rooms at the same time, the shutters, half closed against the sun, clattered open, and, leaning on the wooden balcony, they smiled at one another.

'Wonderful weather!'

'The sea is so smooth, not one little wrinkle!'

'Lucky thing! Have you seen how much the wisteria has grown since last year?'

'And the honeysuckle! Some of the shoots are trapped in the shutters now!'

'Are you going to have a rest, Lily?'

'I'm going to get a jumper and go down. Yes, I can't keep still the first day…What are you going to do, Alice?'

'I'm tidying my linen cupboard. It smells of lavender from last year. You go, I'm enjoying myself enormously. You do what you have to.'

Lily, with a comical gesture, tossed her bleached bob, and a moment later Alice saw her go downstairs, like a green apple into the sandy garden unprotected from the sea breeze.

Alice laughed, not unkindly:

'How plump she is!'

She looked down with satisfaction at her long white fingers and crossed her thin arms on the wooden rail, breathing in the air rich in salt and iodine. The breeze didn't displace one hair of her 'Spanish coiffure', swept back, exposing her forehead and ears, which suited her pretty, regular nose, but was unflattering to all her worsening features: horizontal lines above her eyebrows, drawn cheeks, eyes dark with not sleeping properly. Her friend Lily blamed the severe hairstyle:

'What do you expect? In my opinion fruit that's on the dry side can do with a bit of foliage!'

To which Alice replied:

'Not every forty-year-old can have hair like a girl from the Folies-Bergères!'*

They lived together in perfect harmony and each day their teasing fuelled the fire of their friendship a little more. Alice, elegant and bony, openly admitted:

'My weight hasn't really changed since the year my husband died. Anyway, out of curiosity I kept one of the smocks I wore as a young girl and you'd think it was made yesterday, it fits perfectly!'

Lily had no memories of a marriage, for a very good reason. In her forties, after a wild youth, she had put on weight which was impossible to take off.

'I'm well covered, I know,' she declared. 'But look at my face! no wrinkles! And the rest matches it! That's something, at least, you've got to admit!'

And she shot a spiteful glance at the hollow-cheeked Alice, at the scarf and the fur intended to hide the tendons on the neck and on the T-shaped collarbones.

But it was love, more than rivalry, that bound the two friends one to the other: the same man, handsome, famous, well before he had grown old, had let them down. For Alice, a few letters from the great man were proof that he had taken a fancy to her jealous eyes for a few weeks, her slim, dark, skilfully veiled elegance. Lily had received nothing from him except one wire, but it had been oddly laconic and pressing. A short time later he forgot them both and the 'What, did you know him as well?' of the two friends was followed by half-sincere confidences which they never tired of discussing.

'I didn't understand his sudden silence,' Alice admitted. 'There was a moment in our lives when I'm sure I could have been his friend or spiritual guide, but he went from one to another, nobody could hold on to him.'

'I agree with you, my dear,' responded Lily. 'Friend, guide…I've never understood what those big words mean. All I know is that between him and me…oh my goodness, there was a real spark! Emotions didn't come into it, I tell you! I felt, as clearly as I'm speaking to you now, that I could have had some physical sway over that man. And then the whole thing collapsed. As it always does.'

In short, satisfied with their common disappointments, and having reached the age when women start doing the church flowers, they had hung a portrait, the most lifelike portrait, the one all the newspapers and glossy magazines used, of the reprehensible man in question in the sitting room of Lily's villa, where they were living and sharing the rent for two months. A retouched enlargement in an intense bold black, a fiery etching softened with pink mouth, blue eyes, like a watercolour.

'It's not what you'd call a work of art,' said Alice, 'but when you've known him as I did—as we did, Lily—it's very lifelike!'

For the last two years they had been happily resigned to a sort of religious solitude, seeing inoffensive girlfriends, old, accustomed acquaintances. Growing old? Oh yes, my goodness, growing old, we'd better get used to it. Getting old, beneath the eyes of this youthful portrait, glowing with lovely memories...Getting old with good health, short restful trips out, and small well-chosen meals.

'Don't you think that's preferable to dragging around dance floors, massage parlours, and gaming dens?' Lily said.

Alice nodded but added:

'Everything seems so dull after memories like that...'

Once she had put away her things in the wardrobe, Alice changed her dress, tied a white leather belt around her waist and smiled: 'On the same hole as last year! That's really good news!'

But she felt guilty at not immediately acknowledging *their* portrait in the sitting room downstairs.

'Alice, Alice! Are you coming down?'

Lily's voice downstairs was calling her; she leaned over the wooden balcony:

'Just a minute! What?'

'Come down...Something odd...Come!'

Vaguely excited and always ready for an adventure, she ran down and found Lily in front of 'their' portrait, which had been taken down, placed in full daylight on an armchair.

In the ten months shut away in the dark in the closed villa the exceptional humidity, some combination of salt and colour, had wrought a clever disaster, a work of destruction where chance had equipped itself with an almost miraculous malevolence. On the Roman chin of the celebrity, the damp had drawn the whitish beard of an old man gone to seed. Blisters in the paper made two lymphatic swellings at the top of his cheeks. A few flakes of black charcoal slid down from his hair on to the whole portrait, and made his triumphant face look old and lined. Alice put her white hands over her eyes:

'It's been vandalized!'

Lily, more prosaically, sighed: 'Oh well...' Which said a great deal.

She added, in some agitation:

'We can't leave it there, can we?'

'Oh goodness no, it would make me ill!'

They exchanged glances. Lily thought Alice looked young and slim, and Alice could not help a touch of envy: 'Lily's complexion! Really peachy!'

Their lunch echoed with unwonted chatter, they talked about massages, diets, dresses, and the nearby casino. They spoke, as though incidentally, about the way certain artists tried to stay young, and of their public love affairs. Without apparent motive, Lily cried: 'Hell! Short and sweet? I'd rather it was long and joyful!' and Alice distractedly uttered four or five times the name of the same man, one of their friends who was supposed to spend the summer in that region—'or I am much mistaken'. Their burning desire to escape, full of wicked plans, gave rise to a great deal of eating and drinking, smoking and loose talk. But in the sitting room Alice turned her head aside pityingly when she walked in front of the portrait, and it was the rubicund, frivolous Lily, slightly tipsy, who blew a scornful puff of smoke at the great man's nose:

'Poor old chap!'

THE painter, who intended to do away with himself, made the gesture—both spontaneous and literary—of drafting a short note before he committed suicide. He took a large sheet of Whatman paper* and a pencil, then, just as he was about to write, he changed his mind:

'A short note? But who to? The concierge knows I live on my own, I don't have any family, my girlfriend's left me…We might as well give her the pleasure of telling the tale of this insignificant occurrence, once to the chief inspector, twenty times to the neighbours. My paintings? They can sell them. I could burn them, but I can't be bothered. And the smell of stand oil and charred hemp in this hot weather…Pooh, I don't want my last memory on this earth to smell bad.'

And yet he wasn't sure, he was tormented and agitated like a child with a kind of self-regard and honesty that was very much alive: the need to leave behind him some mark of his passing, a note of the time he vanished, a need which was just as great, in short, as that of expressing his misery at having been betrayed by his girl…He threw down the pencil.

'They'll think I'm asking for pity after I'm dead…so let me die without writing anything! Is it so difficult to simply die?'

He took his revolver, loaded it, felt instinctively with his right arm for the convenient armrest of his large armchair; the soft yellow light of the spring afternoon on the blank canvas on his easel opposite was reflected on his face. He put the weapon down on a small table and got up slowly.

'Yes…I can do it. It's practically an obligation. I see a landscape in myself, it's like my life, it's an explanation for my dying.'

He started to paint rapidly with wide, free brushstrokes unlike his usual style. He scarcely paused to contemplate his internal model, the landscape formed of his youthful, tumultuous suffering, sometimes clear, sometimes swept with clouds that only served, as they passed over, to produce his own blinding clarity and rather conventional symbolism.

He painted a marshy plain, a sort of wild tract of land like those in the Sologne, where separate clumps of blackish-green reeds were immersed in lead-coloured pools. From the foreground, where a few shell-shaped leaves floated like limpets, as far as the horizon, closed by a rigid barrier of cirrus clouds, there was a swamp of bulrushes, a desolate flatness, reflections, wrinkled by the wind, of a sky across which the swell of low clouds was advancing in parallel banks.

In the foreground one single bare tree was bending beneath the gusts of wind, like grasses by the river swaying in obedience to the current. The main branch, broken but still alive, revealed the splintered sapwood beneath the torn bark.

The feverish hand finally came to a halt, the taut arm fell to his side. A warm fatigue was sweetening this last hour of life.

'Good,' said the painter. 'My portrait looks like me. I'm content. Now nothing is stopping me. I'm going to die.'

The rectangular patch of sky beyond the glass bay window was changing from yellow to pink, presaging a long spring twilight. A young woman's voice through a nearby open window began to sing the first notes of such a plaintive, expressive song that the painter, holding his breath, let his glance linger on the window as if he were expecting to see the sounds materialize in copper spheres, in round flowers, in fruit soaked in juice…Revolver in his hand, he leaned curiously out on to the courtyard. He couldn't identify the young voice bidding him such a generous farewell as he approached his death. But from the other side of the yard, in a small dim apartment a blonde nape shone like a sheaf of corn in a dark hayloft.

The painter returned to his canvas, sat down, felt the armrest with his right arm. A long-drawn-out B flat caused the delicate crystal of a nearby glass goblet to vibrate.

'Something's missing on this canvas…Some intervention…some little thing to give it meaning…A detail which would be a simple caption for the picture…'

He put down his revolver and, on the main branch of the tree, began to paint a grey bird, a songbird swelling with melody, turning its head up to the closed firmament and singing.

The painter was pleased with the glossy plumage, a striking pearly jet-black. When evening came and a maidservant brought up his supper, she found the painter standing in front of his canvas beside his forgotten weapon. He had finished painting the bird. Now he was using the last lilac rays of the sun to sketch under the bare tree a still rudimentary flower lifting out of the swamp its sickly and unyielding petal-face.

'IT is certain that we rub shoulders every day with the half-mad; we cannot lock them up like the insane, and we cannot punish them as if they are in normal health. If some people are still unsure about whether the half-mad exist, all they have to do is read the daily newspapers to be convinced.'

Dear Colleague, I invite them too, with the same aim, to edit them out. In June, July, and August the offices where a daily newspaper is put together are snares which lure the half-mad, like a baited mouse-trap. Is it because of our cool landing, our dark hall with the padded doors, the pleasant dampness exuded by the stacks of blank paper? The half-madman, fascinated, seeks out the shade of our offices, bends down to sniff the ink, slake his hidden nervousness on the very source of the tragic event in print which will shortly shock the crowd glued to the displays outside.

But in the main the poor soul arrives encumbered, bloated with disjointed words and already detached from normality, constantly in danger of letting his secret out. He knows he mustn't say anything but his confession trembles on his lips. Stormy or sunny weather increases these malicious attacks, so then he plays with fire, risks the obsessive word in conversation, the tic which reveals all. He's almost always at the mercy of a few syllables, their sounds and shapes make him frantic, and he can control himself as long as he can resist the temptation to utter them once more...again...and just once more...He resists, for his life is nothing but suspicion and concern to keep himself in check. His half-invented conversations, his determination to expound his originality, or political, literary or financial acumen, are not moments of abandon, quite the opposite. He searches out these contacts because he has a taste for risk, distraction and blowing his own trumpet, and in order to prove to himself that he can still chat to us without falling into the deadly intoxication of the repeated word, of the forbidden phrase seething inside him like a flood just held back by the dam, or of the gesture which, once let loose, opens the dread gate to the lunatic asylum.

Since we've had this hot weather, three or four of these unquiet souls lurk around outside the office where I work, find their way in or barge through the door unannounced. One is cordial and lively, with a southern embonpoint, emptying his pockets stuffed with manuscripts, verse and prose that's neither good nor bad. He tells anecdotes, laughs loudly, apologizes for chattering on at me. He is extremely reassuring, except for his habit of lying low for hours on end and then bursting out suddenly with laughter, which gives people less cheerful than him a real fright. But I would still rather have him than the gentle, polite, well-dressed young man who, the first time he appeared, called himself Vernier, the second, Lugard and the third, Wilder. The first thing he did was enquire how one could get a quick divorce, because his free spirit, his ability to work, depended on it. When he called himself Lugard he complained that his family arguments were harming him in his vocation as a painter; finally, the man called Wilder, with the winning, forlorn smile of Lugard, talked sensibly, choosing his words, about his irresistible talents—an original voice, a unique understanding of great musical works—which destined him for the Opéra and the Opéra-Comique. He was obliged to admit in all modesty at the end of our conversation that he didn't know a note of music...One scorching hot day—which one?—will remind me of that young, soft-spoken Proteus with the name of Durand or Bojidar Karageorgevitch. He has charming manners and the sweet face of adolescents who look like their very pretty mothers. No doubt he will be back, disseminating anxiety but preserved by it, having already fled to a place of incurable safety.

Will my stocky visitor with the downy lip, plump as a bubble, blown here by the grumbling gust of a sudden thunderstorm from the west, ever recover? She arrived, talking away nineteen to the dozen, adorned with the graces and attributes of a departmental muse. The olive-green dress, the large, slightly tilted hat, the slinky scarf, the formal gloves, and the manuscript tied up with a curly ribbon—it was all there. Only the shifting light in those puzzling, black, bird-like eyes glimmered in a strange fashion in this overbearing female. This lady of letters began by complaining of the heat, then how difficult it was for a woman without any loss of respectability to get her tales, stories, or novels accepted. In other words, it was a bitter, banal refrain, a rather pointless utterance.

'And yet, Madame, I'm not short of references.'

She brought out the last word harshly, in a shrill, piercing voice and broke off with a nervous laugh.

'I'm sure of that, Madame,' I said. 'And in any case your name is far from being unfamiliar to me...'

My fib made her happy and she gave her roll of manuscript a little shake.

'Is that so? My name is enough to give me a certain standing, a good reference by itself?'

The sound of the word made me shiver, but her prolonged and strident finale seemed to have an even greater effect on the person who had just uttered it for the second time. She recovered her self-possession, untied and unrolled her manuscript which she placed in front of me.

'I am only asking for ten minutes of your time,' she said. 'That's exactly how long it takes to read my first chapter. The first chapter demonstrates the value of the entire work. It contains the scenario of the novel and yet does not take away anything from the volume as a whole.'

She flicked through a score of short, typed pages with her yellow-gloved hand.

'This one is not so good, although it's more striking. It may suit a wider public. This one, twelve short stories...well...I have six hundred and twenty-four if you care to read them...The best, and you will be the judge of that, is this first chapter that sets the scene, the...'

She hesitated before coming out with the word and her face clouded over with a sort of confused, tormented look which made me forget her colour, her plumpness, her shape even, in a mist from whose depths she cried, as though drowning:

'The reference!' Then she closed her eyes for an instant and opened them again in trepidation. I had not moved. She was immediately reassured and grew voluble again.

'I've always thought that detective novels, if you forget about the detective, are an inexhaustible source of tragedy and comedy. You'll see! With only three characters—a young apprentice electrician, an English officer, and a girl, who's not in the least neurotic, oh no, a gay, blonde girl full of...what shall I say? Full of...'

In spite of myself, I muttered:

'References...'

The woman of letters jerked her head back as if I had slapped her and for a second, I waited for some kind of horrific explosion in the peaceful office with the broken blinds. Then she rose, hastily gathered together the papers scattered in front of me and rolled them up again, her eyes, now fine and circumspect, not once leaving my face; she put some space between us and after a brief farewell backed out of the room, mistrustful, in a hurry to escape, like somebody who is truly afraid of the half-mad.

'IT's not an engagement party, no…But no one can be in any doubt. Tomorrow I have to announce to everyone that Claudie Grey is engaged to André Donat, or there'll be a scandal. He's the only boy she's danced with and they've got all our friends on their side. Charles himself…'

Madame Grey looked for her husband and spied him sitting at a poker table. 'There he is running his thumbnail over his lip. Again… and again…and again…Last week I didn't catch him running his thumbnail over his lip once. It's because of this unsettling weather, before the thunderstorm breaks…' She sighed, let her eyes rest on her daughter and on André Donat, who were dancing to the sound of the pianola. Claudie looked like her, as tall and blonde as she had been at the same age.

'Blonde…but it doesn't last very long. That blonde colour turns white quickly, as I very well know. But she looks well this evening. Very well. Worthy of her mother. As for the face, it's uncanny how much she takes after me, in spite of her features being rather smaller. The nose not so long, the eyes not so large, unfortunately; her mouth is not so big as mine, thank goodness…She's pretty. A chip off the old block, as they say. And a good girl…Oh I know it's over and she'll leave me! I'm singing her praises as though…'

Her thoughts broke off abruptly and she superstitiously touched the gold-painted wood of an armchair. Madame Grey loved her only child with the love of an expert, not blind to her faults, but with the kind of critical devotion which creates the bond between the trainer and the champion. Her own good health, her psychological and phys-ical equilibrium had often caused her to be intransigent and severe in the face of female weaknesses she didn't share: 'A migraine? You've got a migraine? Where on earth have you got that from, I've never had a migraine in my life…! A low chignon? Don't be silly, at your age that was the worst hairstyle I had…What suits you is hair piled on top and your nape bare: just look at my portrait by Ferdinand Humbert!'*

Madame Grey adored her when she was a little girl in 1885 in short dresses, with bare legs bathing in the cold water; or a young girl in 1895 on horseback in the Bois, her hair in a ponytail under the black riding-hat; a 'good girl', easy to bring up, rather self-confident, a pedigree filly, a strapping young woman who was never troubled by nerves and wouldn't need to bother three doctors for the birth of her first child.

Madame Grey turned to look at her future son-in-law, with the rancorous expression typical of mothers-in-law.

'Yes, he's a good-looking boy. And he's got it all on a plate, he'll get a house from his papa. This wedding will make a lot of people jealous, for certain. But if I said what I really think, plenty of people wouldn't agree with me...'

André Donat, briefly leaving the tango for the buffet, bowed to Madame Grey as he went by, deposited a light kiss on her hand, tugged her little handkerchief out of her sleeve and escaped, laughing and showing his white teeth. Madame Grey threatened him with her fan and smiled, unamused. She went out on to the terrace, sat down and breathed in the cool dusty night air from the Bois. Her unbending fifty years bent just a little when she was on her own, her knees felt stiff, her strong back muscles longed for bed, for the nice, smooth cotton sheets, the squashy, scalding hot-water bottle.

'That boy makes a point of being nice to me. But how long will it last? When he laughed, he showed his prominent upper front teeth and his little incisors on the lower jaw, too short, as though they've been filed down; his emotions are quick and physical, sensual...I shall be sorry for my daughter if she has pretty maidservants. That nose is too short and lacks judgement...and those earlobes look fused to his cheeks at the back: rather degenerate...And don't forget that when we visited his home, he boasted that he couldn't live in untidiness, that he arranged his books according to their colour on the spine, and that he got out of bed again at night to put his shoes on the shoe tree.'

Madame Grey shivered and got up. In her mind's eye she could see a very young woman standing there, aghast at the sight of a young man in shirt-tails barefoot on the bathroom tiles, admitting with a dreadful, reckless candour that he couldn't sleep if the edges of the towels hanging on the dryer were not lined up at the same height: 'It's funny, darling, because as most things go, I'm rather bohemian, but the edges of the towels...'

'But I can't say that to Claudie,' thought Madame Grey uncomfortably. 'No, I can't. If I tell her that, and that I almost left her father because of him running his nail over his lip, she'd laugh. She wouldn't understand. In any case there are some things you don't tell anyone. You can whisper a few anxious, inept words into a girl's ear on her wedding day. But I could never tell her about the edge of the towels or the thumbnail running over his lip a hundred times or...Oh, enough, enough! She will hide things from me...small, terrible things that blight a marriage, the debris of a man's character abandoned on the verge of childishness and dementia.'

'My poor darling...' Madame Grey sighed. Pulling herself up to her full height, losing in suppleness what she gained in dignity, she went back into the living room. She waved briefly to the engaged couple dancing the Boston and bustled over to the poker table.

'Make room for me, Charles, there are only four of you.'

She had no desire to play poker. But she sat close to her husband and like a good wife, squeezed his hand meaningfully, to warn him about the unconscious fingers running his thumbnail once, twice, a hundred times and then another hundred, over his bottom lip...

His wife touched his shoulder as she went by:

'Do you like the little dancing dolls?'

He didn't much care for this deprecating way of referring to the dancers from Cambodia,* but he gave her a nod and admired his wife as she moved away. She was wearing a silver dress, an artificial rose at her waist, a large fan of artificial feathers, and her hair, skilfully bleached a very light yellow, was like a decoration bought to match the roses and fan. She was a tall woman with a beautiful, somewhat uncomplicated, face, and dominant blue eyes, accustomed to viewing everything critically from her great height.

'The beautiful Madame Issard is splendid this evening,' said a male voice from behind a white silk curtain with beige bamboos painted on it.

'Battledress,' came another voice. 'It's tonight she's hoping to obtain that assignment from the Maréchal for her husband.'

'The assignment wouldn't suit Issard. He's a man of letters. Discerning and home-loving.'

'But it'll suit Madame Issard. Within four months she'll get the rosette for Issard and perhaps the ribbon for herself. Did you hear her when we were having dinner? Magnificent! What diplomacy! And unassailable as well. I must say I don't feel sorry for Issard.'

André Issard moved away from the bamboo curtain. Not that he was afraid of hearing any remark which might upset him about his wife. But he felt the need to have a break from the lengthy adulation of her throughout dinner. Anyway, the Cambodian women, heralded by their tympanums, each one in turn sounding the delicate, liquid note that issues from the throat of toads, were beginning their dance on the stage in front of Pierre Guesde's fifty guests scattered around the hall. From behind his monocle, Issard, somewhat aloof, was enchanted. His notions of the exotic did not stretch beyond Algeria, and he had only seen pictures of Ith, Sarrouth, Trassoth, and their companions in *L'Illustration*. He thought they were pretty but did not care for the ceruse that whitened their round cheeks. He blamed the fashion, introduced from Siam,* for their boyish hairstyles. But beneath this boyish haircut most had slender necks, with no lines or marks, their smooth skin polished, taut, the colour of fine stoneware, or mirabelle plums, ravishing to behold. André Issard tried to think of words that were not too hackneyed to describe those impenetrable childish faces, whose lightly chiselled features—slightly slit eyes, nose hardly extruding from the cheeks, mouths whose short lips revealed their moist red gums inside. With all the obstinacy of the artistic pen-pusher, he was thinking how to describe the curving hands of Sarrouth, her upturned fingers extending an outward-facing palm.

'Like a leaf burnt by autumn? No...more like a fish twisting as it leaps out of water...Or...Yes, I've got it: it's the heraldic curling of a dog's tongue when he's panting.'

Then the music and magic of the undulating movements came together and André Issard had scarcely a thought in his head any more. 'They're pretty...They're original...They are feminine, so feminine...'

He raised his eyes and saw his wife in a deep recess not looking at the dancers but chatting with the governor of a large colony. She was listening, still talking, and seemed to listen as intently as when she spoke. Her eyebrows knitted together, overshadowing her blue eyes with their vision of a glorious, serious future.

'She looks like a man,' André Issard said to himself. 'Why didn't I see that before?'

At the same moment the beautiful Madame Issard, resting her chin in one hand, cupping her elbow in the other, let her eyes roam over the assembled company, seeming to gather powerful admirers here, there, and everywhere in the room. Then she resumed her conversation in a low voice and André Issard noted the oratorical chin, her closed fist tapping out the rhythm of her sentence on the furniture.

'She's a man,' Issard said again to himself, 'I was wondering what it was I had against her...It's that my wife is a man—and what a man! I've only got what I deserve; I should have realized earlier.'

The dancing was coming to an end. He made his way resignedly to the podium where the little dancers, now dispersed, were having to put up with the unkind curiosity of the Europeans. He listened to Pierre Guesde talking in Cambodian to Soun, a singer in the choir, her face not made up, but with black, sparkling eyes and white teeth; he allowed himself to be introduced to Ith, disguised as a Burmese prince, Ith the purity of her features glorified by a hundred photographs; he touched the melting, mobile hands of Sarrouth and while the latter was listening to Pierre Guesde, André Issard kept these passive, cool hands like fleshy leaves in his own. She answered with a little chirping sound, a deferential wave, a childish laugh, and particularly with the words 'Châ...Châ.'

'*Tiâ*,' Issard repeated, imitating Sarrouth's liquid pronunciation. 'What does that mean?'

'That means', Pierre Guesde explained, '*very respectfully, yes*.'

The dancers were leaving. Issard signalled to his wife: 'Shall we go?' She made a scarcely visible, furious sign of *non* in reply. Ten minutes later he was aware of her perfume, the rustle of sequins on her dress.

'The Maréchal is leaving,' she said.

He started:

'I must see him quickly!'

'No,' she said, 'don't. I've fixed up a special meeting for you tomorrow.'

'It would be only polite at least...'

'No,' she replied, 'don't, I said. You can take my word for it. It's all fine. I've sown the seed and sown it well.'

She was steely and radiant as he ushered her towards the exit. In the motor car she called to the driver: 'Go back via the Prado!' and slipped her arm under her husband's, with a sort of cordial condescension, the good humour of a despot. The full moon powdered her pale hair silver and the large artificial feathers on her fan curled like waves in the wind. But André Issard did not see her. He was humming a little tune imitating the Asian music and broke off to murmur under his breath:

'Châ...Châ...'

'What did you say, Dédé?'

He flashed a quick smile at his wife, the look of a rebellious slave:

'Oh nothing! It's a Cambodian word, more or less untranslatable...A word which has no meaning in our language.'

'TWENTY-SEVEN, twenty-eight, twenty-nine…There are definitely twenty-nine.'

Madame Angelier mechanically counted and recounted the little diamond facets. Twenty-nine square jewels set in a bracelet, slithering through her fingers like a thin, cold snake. A pretty connoisseur's piece—the jewels very white and not very large, admirably similar to one another. She fastened it on her arm, causing the diamonds to sparkle in the electric light; a hundred little rainbows glowing with colours danced upon the white cloth. But Madame Angelier's eyes were more especially fixed on that other bracelet, three thinly etched lines circling her wrist above the diamond snake.

'Poor François…if both of us are still here, what's he going to give me next year?'

François Angelier, an industrialist, was currently travelling in Algeria, but whether he was here or not, his present marked the end of the year and their wedding anniversary. Twenty-eight green jade stones last year; the year before, twenty-seven antique mounted enamels…

'And the twenty-six tiny Royal Saxe plates…And the twenty-five metres of antique Alençon lace,' Madame Angelier, with a little effort of memory, could have gone back as far as the four modest silver knives and forks, the three pairs of silk stockings…

'We didn't have much money in those days. Poor François, how he's spoiled me all this time.' Secretly she called him 'Poor François' because she felt guilty for not loving him enough, not recognizing the strength of the habitual tenderness and lasting faithfulness of their marriage.

Madame Angelier raised her hand, bent her little finger, stretched out her wrist to smooth out the bracelet of lines, and said over and over: 'It's so pretty…How shiny the diamonds are…How blest I am…' Then she dropped her hand and admitted to herself that she was already bored by this brand-new piece of jewellery.

'Yet I'm not an ungrateful person,' she sighed naïvely. Her sated eyes wandered from the flowered tablecloth to the sparkling glass case. The smell of the Calville apples in a silver basket made her feel queasy and she left the dining room.

In her boudoir she opened the steel trinket box that contained her jewels and in honour of the new bracelet placed the jewels on her left hand. The ring finger received a ring of black onyx, and a blue diamond; on the little finger delicate, pale, slightly lined, Madame Angelier slipped a ring of dark sapphires. Her prematurely white hair, not tinted, seemed whiter than ever when she placed a narrow bandeau encrusted with a row of diamonds over the gentle waves, and she took it off straight away.

'I don't know what's the matter with me. I'm not myself. But really, it's annoying to be fifty.'

She felt troubled, greedy and disgusted with herself, like a convalescent whose appetite has not yet been restored by the fresh air.

'Anyway, is a diamond as pretty as all that?'

Madame Angelier aspired to visual pleasure intricately flavoured with sensual delight; the unexpected sight of a lemon, the unbearable squeak of the knife as you cut it in half, making you lick your lips in anticipation.

'I don't want a lemon. But that pleasure I can't describe which escapes me, it exists, I know it, I remember it! Like that blue glass bracelet...'

Madame Angelier's slack cheeks tightened as she shivered. A miracle—she couldn't tell how long it lasted—afforded her for a second time the moment she had experienced forty years before, the moment when she had thrilled to the colour of the light, the distorted rainbow image of objects through a band of blue glass made into a bangle that somebody had given her. The glass, possibly oriental, had broken a few hours later but had contained a whole new universe, shapes not imagined in her wildest dreams, pairs of slow-moving serpentine creatures, lamps, frozen rays in an atmosphere of indescribable blue...

The miracle ended and Madame Angelier, bruised, fell back into the present and into reality.

But the very next day she went searching, from antique dealers to flea markets, from flea markets to glassware stores, for a glass bracelet of a particular blue. She searched and searched with a collector's passion, with the thoroughness and secretiveness of an obsessive. She ventured into what she called 'the no-go areas', left her motor car on the corner of unfamiliar streets, and finally, with a few stammered words, bought for a few sous a circle of blue glass which she espied in a dark corner, and carried it off.

Turning up her favourite lamp, she laid the bracelet on the dark surface of a piece of old velvet, leaned over, and waited to experience the thrill. But all she saw was a band of bluish glass, a crude, perhaps a child's, bangle, hastily put together, full of bubbles; an object her memory and her brain recognized as being of the same colour and material; but the powerful and sensual spirit that creates and nourishes a child's visions, and yet so mysteriously fades in us little by little and dies, did not stir.

Resigned, Madame Angelier became conscious of her true age, and of the infinite space beyond which that child, a stranger, would be for ever detached from her, roaming free and even defying the command of memory: a little girl of ten who used to wear on her wrist a bracelet of blue glass.

THE setting sun touched the curtains, crossed the salon from one end to the other, and Irène's friends cried out in admiration.

'It's magical!'

'What a find! Unique!'

'And the Seine all lit up!'

'The sky's growing pink...'

One friend, more honest than the rest, murmured vindictively, taking in the Seine, the ancient salon leading into a rustic dining room, the purple and silver curtains, the orange cups, and the wood fire:

'It's so unfair!'

And poor little Madame Auroux, who had divorced in order to marry again and was unable to because she couldn't find an apartment, had such genuine tears in her blue eyes that Irène gave her a hug:

'You shouldn't be in a hurry to do such a silly thing again, my dear. Actually, I think it's the divorce that brought me luck. I tell you, it was a lucky chance finding this little gem.'

Irène, who would not have dared flaunt a sparkling new ring in front of an indigent friend, was showing off her beautiful home with immodest pride. She stretched her arms out, and, as though confiding a guilty secret:

'Oh my dears, if you knew how lovely the mornings are here! These boats, these reflections of the water dancing on the ceiling...'

But they'd had enough. Bitterly envious and in any case replete with cakes, they all left together. Leaning on the wrought-iron ramp, 'a jewel from the eighteenth century, my dear!' Irène cried 'Au revoir! Au revoir!', waving her hand as though she were on the steps of a château. She went back in, walked over, and pressed her forehead against the window. A brief winter twilight was rapidly blotting out the pink and gold of the sky reflected in the water and the bright twinkling of the evening star foretold a frosty night.

Behind her, Irène heard the clatter of cups being collected by over-hasty hands as her maid scurried around. She turned:

'Are you in a hurry, Pauline?'

'It's not that, Madame, but I have my husband...It's Saturday and as Madame knows, they have the whole weekend off.'

'Do go! You can do the dishes tomorrow. No, don't lay a place for me, I had so much tea I shan't want anything to eat this evening.'

Since moving house she'd had to put up with hurried dinners, or cold meats from the nearby charcuterie, because Pauline, the home help who did all the housework, lived out. Some evenings when she had a lot to do, Irène donned a blue apron, grilled a piece of gammon herself, and broke two eggs into a buttered pan.

She heard the door slam shut and Pauline go downstairs in her clogs. A tram hummed along its rails on the opposite platform. The house, old and solidly built, hardly registered at all when the carriages went past, and the barking of the neighbour's dog or the piano from the floor above did not penetrate the thick walls. Irène put another log on the fire, and, around the fireplace—'an authentic *cheminée coquille*,* my dear!'—arranged the little table that served as a desk, the big armchair, the books, the folding screen, and then stood contemplating the decor of her happiness...The regular chiming of a clock could be heard outside.

'Seven o'clock. Only seven o'clock. Still thirteen hours till tomorrow.'

She gave a small shudder, humbled before the inanimate witnesses—the purple curtains, the monument which rose up into the night sky like the prow of a steamer, the unused armchair, and the book whose spell over her was broken—and abandoning that state of being a fortunate woman of whom it is said that she has a 'quiet life' and a 'unique apartment'.

No more spouse getting in the way and leaving the house in a mess, no more scenes, no more unexpected returns home, exits that seemed like escapes, suspicious telegrams, invisible females on the end of the phone being addressed as 'my dear chap' or 'my dear sir'.

No more husband, no children, admirers but not lovers...'Free as a bird!' her jealous friends exclaimed.

'But did I ask to be free and take flight, I wonder?'

She had got back her dowry and recovered her independence, moved into an old luxurious lodging, light and hidden away, ideal for a recluse or a couple in love, and was now enjoying the quiet life—oh so quiet...!

'But did I really need such a quiet life?'

Beneath the ceiling that was too high Irène was still standing in front of the easy chair and screen that were trying to tighten round her a refuge that would fit. She felt a keen desire for light, lit the little lamp of smoked glass with antique bronze arms and the basket of electric fruits on the dining-room table. But she left unlit the bedroom she had been so proud of before, with her Spanish bed, with the four gilt wooden flames in the four corners rising like heraldic pales...

'My house is lovely,' she acknowledged dispassionately. 'Now all I have to do is wait to show it to my other friends. Then what?'

She could see herself day after day enthusing like a tourist guide over the mantelpiece with the shell decoration, the wrought-iron rail, the Seine, the wood that had lost its gilt...Suddenly she had a violent desire for a little furnished room like the one where, for lack of anything better, a friend was living with a young painter, a small studio littered with cigarette ash, splashes of coloured paint, but alive with quarrels, laughter, reconciliations. At the same time she felt an almost physical surge of longing mixed with bitter regret for a studio that would double as an apartment—you had to live somewhere!—for a whole family, two parents, three beautiful children all resembling one another, three little pure-bred puppies. The warmth of the narrow, sensuous room, the daylight falling through the studio straight down on to three small, naked bodies...Irène abruptly put out the light and breathed a quick sigh of relief when the lovely antique decor of the apartment disappeared. She moved the screen and the armchair away from the fire, drew the curtains, put on an old warm coat, cautiously and disapprovingly extinguished the last lamp in the salon and left, taking with her a detective novel, caviar sandwiches and a dish of chocolate, to finish her evening sunk into a basket chair in the bathroom squeezed in between the shower and the washbasin.

It's not that I particularly like it in here, but it's so cold outside. Here, the air wraps you round like feathers in an eiderdown as soon as you step inside. When I was a child, I slept in the winter under an enormous cloud of goose feathers, imprisoned in the red taffeta of a special light eiderdown that emitted a mysterious sort of radiant warmth. In this place you simply can't breathe. But you absorb all the aromas of a *salon de thé*. Frangipane, baked pastry, the bitter vegetable taste of burnt tea, *baba au rhum*,* a carbonized crumb of toast fallen in the ash, and especially perfumes, women's perfumes. No sanctions against certain perfumers exist, the fabrication of essences is dangerously unregulated, the female sense of smell is often undeveloped, unsophisticated, women scramble to try everything in perfume bottles. Lavender thinned down with angelica, rose sticky with geranium, extract of vanilla uselessly tonified with resin, tarry narcissus, lilac with prussic acid, carnation with creosote, benzoin disguised as amber, and all those unidentifiable blooms, the distillation of beds of flowers where you inevitably detect the intrusive, sickly essence of wild parsnip!

I try and ignore the perfumes which float around and clash with one another. My two neighbours are pretty, they smell nice. But I would find the brunette's sandalwood cloying after a while and I know that behind the 'red rose' that the blonde sprayed herself with, behind the olfactories there's a subtle fetid note of fresh ink. But no matter. We are not going to spend our lives together, the brunette, the blonde and I.

The brunette is pretty and the bleached blonde attractive. But the brunette, all in grey velvet with flame-coloured pearly panels, a silver fox fur round her neck and spangled shoes with feathers and rhinestones, embroidered gloves with piping, and with a haze of feathers in her hair which looks like a threatening thunderstorm over her two starry eyes, the brunette radiates that rather hard style of elegance that is so popular nowadays. Women stop eating and chatting as she comes in. They watch her, and the envious looks add to her beauty, just as the summer rain enhances the enamel lustre of a kingfisher. She's thirsty, she drinks like a pigeon, stretching out her neck with her drooping jabot. She has two gestures, as frequent as nervous tics, but which are in fact deliberate, provocative movements: with her first finger she pushes back a very light brown curl from her forehead, and you see the almond-shaped fingernail close to her elongated eye; at the nape of her neck she secures a shell-shaped, three-pronged comb, and when she raises her arm, your eyes follow the rounded, well-supported bosom that lifts again at the same time as the arm.

The blonde...the blonde is charming in her own way. Only a blonde, in black Moroccan crêpe and velvet cape, a blonde with a short neck, a voracious mouth. Her little nervous tics don't do anything for her. Her chin sticks out like a bulldog's and she turns up her nose like a little seal popping up out of the sea, blinking. It's not pretty—I'd like to tell her so...Well, too bad! And now she's imitating the gestures of her friend, with everyone's eyes on her. She sticks out her bust, with one hand pats her low, gold chignon. A younger sister often unconsciously in that manner imitates an older one, who is already confident of her attractiveness. What fun it is observing these two self-assured peahens! The more beautiful woman looks down a little on the more docile one and the latter, not without a twinge of jealousy, imitates, complies, corrects herself.

A man appears. Were they expecting him? I believe so. For with one voice they exclaim: 'Oh!' as though surprised. Which one has he come for? I can't tell. One fills his cup, the other offers him a cake. Impartial, courteous, he leans towards the blonde, then directs all his attention to what the brunette is saying. I have the impression that the blonde is irritated, she thrusts out her jaw, wrinkles her nose, laughs too loudly. Now she looks ugly next to her rival...The man has eyes only for the brunette, her grey and flame-coloured dress, her pale face, her pink index finger, her rounded breast which manifests a life of its own beneath her bodice. I'm betting on the brunette...and I've lost! The man turns imperceptibly, ineluctably, towards the blonde. First his body slowly leans in her direction. Then the chair shifts, with little impatient movements. The blonde may thrust out her chin as much as she likes, may make that rather coarse gesture which shortens her neck, she may screw up her nose and display too much of her gums above her crooked teeth, it doesn't matter now how she behaves. The man likes her best. She wins, and in an instant she is blushing, like a piece of fruit touched by a ray of dawn.

And the brunette, agitated, unsure, intervenes, trying to discover the secret of this victorious blonde, even going so far as to imitate her, wrinkling up her nose, fluttering her eyelids and grimacing like a mastiff, with her jaw stuck out and baring her teeth...

THEY quarrelled as they had become friends, without knowing why. But what's certain is that Jeannine, laughing overenthusiastically, had told others Andrée's real name, her grandmother having named her Symphorienne when she was baptized. Another version of the story is that Andrée, tactlessly exaggerating her authority as the elder, and a strapping, dark-haired beauty into the bargain, had, after twenty cups of tea and as many glasses of port, indicated to Jeannine that it was time to leave, by whistling her much as she whistled her dogs in the Bois de Boulogne. Impartial for once, friends sat on the fence and blamed both Jeannine and Andrée: 'You can't be sure that Andrée whistled Jeannine, but such coarseness would be very typical of her; that stupid Jeannine is very good at acting the underdog, just for the sadistic pleasure of snivelling in humiliation later.'

Once they had quarrelled, they bore with both dignity and discretion the period of mourning after the demise of their close friendship, which had lasted through two trips to Deauville, two to Chamonix, and three to the Riviera. Jeannine, the weaker one, the more brazen and flighty, changed her dance venue, found a new little café in Belleville where she went to drink tea in the afternoon with her friends, and again at one o'clock in the morning to eat potato salad and that strange creature, the garfish, popular in flea markets but shunned in upper-class fish shops because of its jade green backbone. Without Jeannine, Andrée returned to her favourite rustic pursuits, went walking in the Bois, and canoeing on the lake an hour earlier. 'I'll drown my sorrows,' Jeannine thought, and Andrée with her sensible shoes, her balaclava, and her hands in her pockets, just kept saying: 'Don't talk to me about close friends, men or women! I'm turning into the wild nymph of the virgin forest again!' When it came down to it, they accepted with a naïve surprise their mutual indifference and the marvellous ease and non-threatening nature of their separation.

Spring brought Jeannine back to the restaurants in the Bois de Boulogne. May saw her shivering in a cape of white crêpe, dancing to warm up at eleven at night on a parquet floor whitened by the light of an electric moon between the tables and saplings flapping in the icy wind. She crossed the Bois de Boulogne every time a day's shopping allowed her to show off in the fickle sunshine her winter gauzes followed by summer furs. But whether it was day or night, this Bois did not remind her of her friend the nymph, for the morning Bois and its walkers do not bear any resemblance to the evening Bois and its motor cars.

One day, however, when she was on her own, at the unaccustomed time of a quarter to twelve, she chanced to cross one of the long paths that lead from the Entre Deux Lacs to the Cascade. She walked quickly, because her new close friend, a sporty girl, had just decided to play tennis instead, and Jeannine, feeling let down, had refused to drive her there. She walked, but took no pleasure in it, didn't hear the nightingales, nor the thrushes and orioles that try to imitate the nightingales. The acacias, losing their blossoms, were snowing unnoticed at Jeannine's feet, her pert little nose, imperious, like a swift's beak, impervious to their scent of vanilla doughnuts and orange blossom.

A whistle brought her up short, and she knew why when she heard someone shout through the woods: 'Come on, little doggies!' A German shepherd dog appeared, just long enough let her see the ursine eyes, and low bushy tail of a she-wolf. A bulldog followed, snorting like an ancient taxicab, white and with a black half-moon monocle, and after that a frantic yellow griffon with hair bristling like stubble.

'Mieke…Relaps…Joli-Blond…' Jeannine counted them. Behind the dogs Andrée crossed the path and didn't see Jeannine, who recognized the chestnut-coloured raincoat, the muddy flat-heeled boots, the red woollen scarf, and the whip with the large, plaited handle.

'Come on little doggies!'

The shout faded away; one of the dogs barked in the distance. Jeannine stood still, trembling. Still hoping for the familiar call, no longer hearing anything, she stumbled along the path again, faltering, her face ashen, her eyes blinking away two obstinate tears.

'I don't know…I really don't know what's come over me…'

For her heart did not leap out to Andrée. Without emotion, she imagined the smell of her perfume 'a bit like a harem' and her virile hand in the large glove. But deep inside there was a jealous tenderness, a regret, stinging like the pain of a child, that was badly wanting those three dogs eager for their walk, wanting the pleasure of calling them by their names, the right to make the mark of two high heels on the wet path next to two low heels of rubber boots; the privilege of making, to the mist on the lake, to the wide-open blooms of the elder-flower, to the branch laden with blue tits, silly little remarks, only worth saying at that moment, the sweet, foolish tradition, the safety of knowing they would be repeated the next day.

Being alone made her lose heart. She gave way to a soft groan as she walked along, muttering incoherently like a child:

'I want the dogs...I want the morning...I want to get up early... I want warm milk with rum in the kiosk by the lake, the day when it didn't stop raining...I want...'

She turned round, waiting for Andrée or the dogs to come back along the path, to restore the image of a time that from now on would be inaccessible to her, and quickly found the formula for her wishes and the expression of her distress:

'I want it to be last year...'

EXPLANATORY NOTES

THE CAT

4 *Mistinguett*: professional name of the actress and singer Jeanne Florentine Bourgeois (1873–1956), arguably the most popular female French entertainer of her day and at one point the highest-paid female entertainer in the world.

5 *Neuilly*: a select residential suburb of Paris, close to the Bois de Boulogne. Successive waves of affluent Parisians have chosen to live in Neuilly: Alain's family are long-established residents whereas Camille's are 'new money'.

6 *Quart-de-Brie*: Alain and Camille call their flat 'the Quarter of a Brie' because its triangular structure resembles a quarter of the large round cheese.

9 *brocatelle*: 'an imitation of brocade, usually made of silk or wool, used for tapestry, upholstery' (*Oxford English Dictionary*).

10 *Chartreux*: a rare pedigree breed of cat, originally from France, known for its silver-grey fur, quiet intelligence, and hunting skills. Chartreux cats have a tendency to bond with one person. Colette herself owned a series of Chartreux cats.

14 *biscottes*: crispbreads, long popular in France as a breakfast food.

17 *'She called me vous in those days'*: *vous* is the more formal mode of address in French, implying respect, as opposed to the informal *tu*.

22 *banlieue*: the suburbs, the outer areas of the city.

27 *caravansérail... capharnaüm*: Alain's mother mixes up the words. The first means a place of rest built in the desert; the second means a place containing a jumble of objects in disarray.

43 *Marie Dubas*: music-hall singer, 1894–1972.

Loïsa Puget: composer, 1810–89.

52 *son of Penelope and a tortoise*: Camille is referring to Telemachus, who in Homer's *Odyssey*, spends a long time wandering the world looking for his father, Odysseus.

56 *Folie-Saint-James*: an eighteenth-century landscape garden in Neuilly.

62 *Whatmann paper*: high-quality woven paper used for drawing or printing, named for its inventor James Whatman (1702–59).

65 *Les donneurs... de sé-é-rénades, Et les bel-les é-écouteu[ses]*...: 'The givers of serenades and their beautiful listeners...' These are the opening lines of the poem 'Mandoline' by Paul Verlaine (1844–96), set to music by several composers, including Claude Debussy (1862–1918), Gabriel Fauré (1845–1924), and Reynaldo Hahn (1874–1947). Colette's use of hyphens and suspension dots in the text suggests she is referring to the setting by Fauré. I am grateful to Rowena Anketell for this information.

THE MASKED WOMAN

92 *Extension Économique*: literally 'Economic Extension', suggesting a journal devoted to economic affairs. Colette invented the title, or was possibly thinking of *L'Expansion économique*, published in France from 1917 to 1925.

94 *pannes bénies*: a play on words—*le pain bénit* (literally 'blessed bread') is the holy wafer, or host. *Une panne* is a breakdown when driving.

Scola Cantorum: a private music academy in Paris set up in the late nineteenth century.

96 *causeuses*: small sofas for two people.

101 *la vie à deux*: literally 'a life for two', meaning living as a couple.

104 *Auteuil*: a pleasant Parisian suburb, part of the 16th *arrondissement* (see note to p. 118).

105 *Tantalus*: in Homer's *Odyssey*, Tantalus offended the gods and was condemned to Hades where his punishment was to be forever thirsty, though standing in a pool of water that flowed away from him whenever he tried to drink, and hungry, though close to a fruit tree, the fruit of which the wind wafted away each time he tried to eat it.

106 *Les Halles*: the central fresh food market in Paris until 1973.

108 *à la chinoise*: 'Chinese style'; that is, drawn back smoothly and tightly into a low chignon.

110 *nègre en chemise*: dessert made with chocolate, butter, eggs, and sugar, popular in France in the 1920s and 1930s. Its title has become problematic since *nègre* is a racist term for a black person.

111 *the Müller method*: a system of exercises, fashionable in the early twentieth century, to improve muscle tone and general dexterity. First published by J. P. Müller in 1904.

115 *chapeau de Mercure*: a fashionable style of hat. Mercury, messenger of the gods, is usually pictured wearing a winged helmet.

118 *the Council*: the Council of Ministers, or Cabinet.

arrondissement... quartier: *arrondissement* is an administrative division. Paris is divided into twenty *arrondissements*, each of which is divided into four *quartiers*, though the word *quartier* has also come to mean simply 'district' or 'neighbourhood'.

122 *toile de Jouy*: cloth printed with a coloured motif of bucolic scenes, by the 1920s implying a pretty but old-fashioned style.

126 *chalets normands*: 'chalet' suggests a house built in cottage style with a sloping roof, presumably a style associated with Normandy.

133 *Folies-Bergères*: one of the most famous Parisian music halls, it opened in 1869 and was renowned for its revues featuring semi-nude chorus girls. The careers of many famous French stars, including Josephine Baker and Maurice Chevalier, were launched there.

137 See note to p. 62.

143 *Ferdinand Humbert*: French painter (1842–1931) who specialized in portraits. He painted Colette herself when she was married to Willy, around 1896.

146 *dancers from Cambodia*: the Cambodian National Ballet had appeared in Paris and Marseilles in 1906, and were famously drawn by the artist and sculptor Auguste Rodin. They returned to France for the 1922 Colonial Exposition, again to great public acclaim—thus the allusion is topical.

Siam: the official name for Thailand until 1939.

153 *cheminée coquille*: antique marble mantelpiece with a scallop shell carving.

155 *salon de thé... baba au rhum*: *salon de thé* is a tearoom or smart café; *baba au rhum*, a small yeast cake soaked in syrup and rum, usually filled with whipped cream.

The Oxford World's Classics Website

www.oxfordworldsclassics.com

- Browse the full range of Oxford World's Classics online

- Sign up for our monthly e-alert to receive information on new titles

- Read extracts from the Introductions

- Listen to our editors and translators talk about the world's greatest literature with our Oxford World's Classics audio guides

- Join the conversation, follow us on Twitter at OWC_Oxford

- Teachers and lecturers can order inspection copies quickly and simply via our website

www.oxfordworldsclassics.com

American Literature

British and Irish Literature

Children's Literature

Classics and Ancient Literature

Colonial Literature

Eastern Literature

European Literature

Gothic Literature

History

Medieval Literature

Oxford English Drama

Philosophy

Poetry

Politics

Religion

The Oxford Shakespeare

A complete list of Oxford World's Classics, including Authors in Context, Oxford English Drama, and the Oxford Shakespeare, is available in the UK from the Marketing Services Department, Oxford University Press, Great Clarendon Street, Oxford OX2 6DP, or visit the website at www.oup.com/uk/worldsclassics.

In the USA, visit www.oup.com/us/owc for a complete title list.

Oxford World's Classics are available from all good bookshops.

A SELECTION OF   **OXFORD WORLD'S CLASSICS**

JOHN BUCHAN   **Huntingtower**
                               The Thirty-Nine Steps

JOSEPH CONRAD   **Heart of Darkness and Other Tales**
                               Lord Jim
                               Nostromo
                               The Secret Agent
                               Under Western Eyes

FORD MADOX FORD   **The Good Soldier**

JOHN GALSWORTHY   **The Forsyte Saga**

JAMES JOYCE   **A Portrait of the Artist as a Young Man**
                               Dubliners
                               Occasional, Critical, and Political
                                    Writing
                               Ulysses

RUDYARD KIPLING   **The Jungle Books**
                               Just So Stories
                               Kim
                               War Stories and Poems

D. H. LAWRENCE   **The Rainbow**
                               Sons and Lovers
                               Women in Love

WYNDHAM LEWIS   **Tarr**

KATHERINE MANSFIELD **Selected Stories**

ROBERT TRESSELL   **The Ragged Trousered Philanthropists**

VIRGINIA WOOLF   **Flush**
                               The Mark on the Wall and Other Short
                                    Fiction
                               Mrs Dalloway
                               Orlando: A Biography
                               A Room of One's Own and Three Guineas
                               To the Lighthouse

W. B. YEATS   **The Major Works**

ANTON CHEKHOV	About Love and Other Stories
	Early Stories
	Five Plays
	The Princess and Other Stories
	The Russian Master and Other Stories
	The Steppe and Other Stories
	Twelve Plays
	Ward Number Six and Other Stories
FYODOR DOSTOEVSKY	Crime and Punishment
	Devils
	A Gentle Creature and Other Stories
	The Idiot
	The Karamazov Brothers
	Memoirs from the House of the Dead
	Notes from the Underground and The Gambler
NIKOLAI GOGOL	Dead Souls
	Plays and Petersburg Tales
MIKHAIL LERMONTOV	A Hero of Our Time
ALEXANDER PUSHKIN	Boris Godunov
	Eugene Onegin
	The Queen of Spades and Other Stories
LEO TOLSTOY	Anna Karenina
	The Kreutzer Sonata and Other Stories
	The Raid and Other Stories
	Resurrection
	War and Peace
IVAN TURGENEV	Fathers and Sons
	First Love and Other Stories
	A Month in the Country

ANTHONY TROLLOPE

The American Senator
An Autobiography
Barchester Towers
Can You Forgive Her?
Cousin Henry
Doctor Thorne
The Duke's Children
The Eustace Diamonds
Framley Parsonage
He Knew He Was Right
Lady Anna
The Last Chronicle of Barset
Orley Farm
Phineas Finn
Phineas Redux
The Prime Minister
Rachel Ray
The Small House at Allington
The Warden
The Way We Live Now

SHERWOOD ANDERSON	**Winesburg, Ohio**
WILLA CATHER	**O Pioneers!**
JAMES FENIMORE COOPER	**The Last of the Mohicans**
STEPHEN CRANE	**The Red Badge of Courage**
THEODORE DREISER	**Sister Carrie**
W. E. B. DU BOIS	**The Souls of Black Folk**
F. SCOTT FITZGERALD	**The Beautiful and Damned** **The Great Gatsby**
BENJAMIN FRANKLIN	**Autobiography and Other Writings**
CHARLOTTE PERKINS GILMAN	**The Yellow Wall-Paper and Other Stories**
NATHANIEL HAWTHORNE	**The Scarlet Letter**
HENRY JAMES	**The Portrait of a Lady** **The Turn of the Screw and Other Stories**
JACK LONDON	**The Call of the Wild** **White Fang and Other Stories**
HERMAN MELVILLE	**Billy Budd, Sailor and Selected Tales** **Moby-Dick**
EDGAR ALLAN POE	**Selected Tales**
HARRIET BEECHER STOWE	**Uncle Tom's Cabin**
HENRY THOREAU	**Walden**
MARK TWAIN	**Adventures of Huckleberry Finn** **The Adventures of Tom Sawyer**
EDITH WHARTON	**The Custom of the Country** **Ethan Frome**
WALT WHITMAN	**Leaves of Grass**